Fishermen, Carpenters, Mechanics, and Tax Collectors

A layman's guide to fulfilling the Great Commission

Glen D. Pierce

© 2015 by Glen D. Pierce

All rights reserved. No part of this publication may be reproduced in any form without the prior written consent of the author, except for brief quotations in printed reviews.

Published by CrossVision Missions INT
P.O. Box 132982
Tyler, TX 75713

ISBN - 13: 978-0692626023
ISBN - 10: 0692626026

Unless otherwise indicated, Scripture quotations are from The ESV Bible (The Holy Bible, English Standard Version), copyright © 2001 by Crossway, a publishing ministry of Good News Publishers. Used by permission. All rights reserved.

Scripture quotations labeled "The Message" are taken from the "THE MESSAGE", © 1993, 1994, 1995, 1996, 2000, 2001, 2002. Used by permission.

Contents

Preface 7

PART 1 13

    Chapter 1 Confirming Spiritual Birth 15

    Chapter 2 Understanding the Relationship 29

    Chapter 3 A Child of God 47

PART 2 57

    Chapter 4 The Blessed Attitudes 59

    Chapter 5 The Visible Righteous Life 81

    Chapter 6 Making Righteous Choices and Decisions . 87

PART 3 101

    Chapter 7 Living an Evangelistic Lifestyle 103

PART 4 119

    Chapter 8 Getting Started Making Disciples 121

PERSONAL CHALLENGE 147

Suggested Study 151

Preface

I grew up sitting on the front row of small country churches. My dad was a lay preacher and seldom did a Sunday pass that he was not preaching as an interim in a pulpit somewhere. Being in church was all I knew. I believed it was what all good Christians were supposed to do. I can't remember not being an active member in the church. However, the fact is that I, like most Christian kids, didn't have a clue what having a relationship with Jesus really meant. One day in my late twenties, I was serving on a brotherhood team repairing a widow woman's house. Robert, a man slightly older than me, asked me if I was truly a disciple. I answered, "Sure I am!" The truth was, I didn't even understand why he would ask me this question. The more I tried to forget it, the more it echoed through my mind.

Out of a need to find out if my dad and the preachers were telling the truth when they said a disciple is simply a student learning from a teacher, I soon began to ask others the same question. The more I asked the more certain I became that there is much more to being a disciple than I knew. I felt like getting to the basic teachings of Christ was like a scavenger hunt through the Land of Oz.

This set me on a path to discover what a true disciple really is. The process God has carried me through has been incredible. It has brought me to this point in my life where God has challenged me not to let others go through life as good Christians who never know the close, personal, identifiable, and contagious relationship a disciple has with Jesus.

The Bible teaches us that Jesus developed a close, personal relationship with a handful of common, hardworking, God-fearing men that He found to be trustworthy and teachable. After a year and a half of training them for the task of evangelizing the world, He gave them one instruction: Go make disciples. In no way did Jesus intend this assignment to be taken as an individual challenge. He knew that the task of making disciples would require them to go, minister, and grow future disciples together. Jesus knew if He gave them individual tasks, it would ultimately divide them. Listen to how Paul describes what we look like as a disciple-making team: "For as in one body we have many members and the members do not all have the same function, so we, though many, are one body in Christ, and individually members of one another." (Romans 12:4-5.)

It could be that you are in the same place I was the day Robert confronted me with that question and you have never taken a hard look at your own spiritual position in Christ; or you may be like the hundreds of Christians I have encountered who want with all their hearts to be disciple makers but simply do not know where or how to start. For this, as well as other reasons, God has compelled me to share my story with others in the hope that my journey to make disciples, along with a very simple guide to making disciples, will enable some followers of Christ to begin to see themselves as a part of the disciple-making process.

My story is very similar to that of many Christians and yet it is unique to me at the same time. Through my research, and now years of asking challenging questions to fellow believers, I have realized that many faithful church members have no understanding of the great commission of Christ. Even though some might see what I am saying as an attack on the church, I never had in my mind that I could effect a change in how we do church, but I firmly believe, and statistics prove, that if we do not change the way we do church, local church congregations will continue to die out.

What about you and your church? Can I ask some very candid questions? Does the number of members equal a successful disciple-making ministry? Do high numbers of baptisms equal fulfilling the great commission of Christ? Where in the Gospels do we see Jesus demonstrate the art of mass discipleship?

Somehow evangelical Christians have determined that all disciple making is the job of the pastor and his staff. Most laymen would not admit this truth, but if we ask them how they go about making disciples, they simply clam up or talk about the one guy they invited to church some time ago. If we ask pastors, they will say, "We are truly a disciple-making church. We have a great outreach, a tremendous men's ministry and an even stronger women's ministry. Our children and youth ministries are second to none." Yet, if we press them by asking, "Who in your church have you seen blossom into full-fledged disciple makers," their answers will be dampened by the truth that it is a small fraction of their congregations. And although the pastor's efforts will be wholehearted and full of desire for his church to be disciple makers, few within the congregation will earnestly accept their responsibility to be the small part of the body that works and serves for the benefit of the other parts of the body.

My journey, coming from the view in the pew has enabled me to see and understand a few basic truths that for one reason or another have failed to be understood or incorporated into the daily lives of the vast majority of faithful church members today. In my pursuit of God and a truly personal relationship with Him, the truths of spiritual birth and how every relationship with God the Father works, including Jesus' relationship with the Father, has caused me to begin to live the life of a disciple and come to realize that helping others discover their own personal relationship with God is really what disciple making is all about.

I know my life is not as unique as some might want to think and, if we get real about our lives in Christ, we will find that most, like myself, have never truly been a part of a fully functional disciple-making church. As a result, an epidemic of church hopping and young people rebelling against their parents' beliefs has choked the future of evangelical disciple making. Today young people flock to high energy, emotionally-charged services and view it as the evolution of church into a more sinner-friendly place to hangout. At the same time, the 40-plus generations are growing weary of the one-man domination and pass-the-plate routine typical of Sunday morning. I am not speaking as an outsider looking in, but rather as one who has watched his peers and friends fall away from church or simply become duty oriented and satisfied with a once-a-week, 30-minute fill up on Sunday morning.

As I began to minister to church dropouts as well as young people in search of a quick charge without any commitment, I learned some common threads that affected the spiritual understanding and personal relationship of almost all church members as well as a huge problem in the way most people present the gospel. When I re-evaluated the way I shared the Gospel, I was forced to make some hard changes and drop the sinner's prayer as my ultimate goal. I had to face the fact that Jesus does not commission us to plant seeds or make converts. Jesus very clearly commissioned us to make disciples.

The absolute truth is that getting to the basic teachings of Christ *shouldn't* be like a scavenger hunt through the Land of Oz. This book, as well as *The Carpenter's Four-Part Guide to Making Disciples*, that I have developed for laymen and women, has come from my personal relationship with Christ as a disciple maker. God put it in my heart to speak to the person who loves the Lord Jesus and wants to understand how His great commission relates to them personally, both the believer who has never really understood his life as a child of God, and the faithful church member who wants to understand more about his personal relationship with Jesus, how we talk to Him, how we love Him and how we please Him. God never intended for us to be individual disciple makers, but He did intend for all of His children to be an active part of the disciple-making process. What we need the most is a guide, a person to help us get started, to help us understand that it is not about our head knowledge, but rather it's all about God using our contagious, personal relationship with Jesus to draw others into a personal disciple's relationship with Him.

PART 1

Are You Truly a
Disciple of Christ Jesus?

"All authority has been given to me, go and make disciples of all nations…"
~Jesus Christ
(Matt. 28:18-19)

Chapter 1

Confirming Spiritual Birth

"Truly, truly, I say to you, unless one is born again he cannot see the Kingdom of God."
~Jesus
(John 3:3)

How many times have you heard someone, a politician, an actor, or maybe even one of your family members say, "I am born again," yet you know in your heart if they were asked to even spell the word spiritual they would lose the spelling bee? They claim what they have only heard about and there is no visible proof in their life. The truth is, to most people, it's a term that makes the Christians in the room comfortable. It is used as loosely as the name Jesus, and few ever take time to discover if they really have experienced spiritual birth. I love the way Eugene Peterson describes Spiritual Birth in his paraphrase of the Bible, *THE MESSAGE*:

"Jesus said, you're not listening. Let me say it again. Unless a person submits to this

original creation – the 'wind-hovering-over-the-water' creation, the invisible moving the visible, a baptism into a new life – it's not possible to enter God's kingdom. When you look at a baby, it's just that: a body you can look at and touch. But the person who takes shape within is formed by something you can't see and touch – the Spirit – and becomes a living spirit." (John 3:5-6)

We don't fully understand the spiritual birth that Jesus tells Nicodemus he doesn't have, but one thing we can know for certain is that there are evidences that it has happened and those who have been born of the Spirit can see and, in fact, live in the Kingdom of God here and now.

So what does **spiritual birth** really look like? How do we know for sure we have it? And if we are to help others identify their spiritual birth, what do we look for? I ate lunch a couple of times of week with my good friend and prayer partner, Bill, who owned a transmission repair business. As I walked into the shop one day, his head mechanic, Richard, called me over. He told me he was having marital problems and wanted to know if I would be willing to talk with him and his wife. I replied, "I don't know what I can do, but I would be glad to talk with you." He was at work, so I told him to name the time and place and I would be there. Bill and I went on to lunch.

I had no idea how pressing the burden was on Richard, but when I returned from lunch, he and his wife were standing by the bay door waiting for me. It was his lunch hour so we had plenty of time to talk. I simply asked, "Tell me where you are with Jesus."

Richard began to describe how he had grown up in church and how he and his wife had been members of a local church until the pastor required each member to pay for new chairs in the auditorium and they began to walk away from God. Richard had begun to drink daily and she had become a weekend bar hopper. Together they had made partying and drinking all but a religious practice. In short, alcohol and their party friends were in control of their lives.

Richard said, "I'm sick of myself and I'm sick of this life." His wife followed with, "But we don't know how to get out of it." The first thing I needed to help them realize was that their lives gave no evidence that they had ever put their faith in Jesus as Lord of their lives. For them to be able to put their faith in Jesus and truly let Him be Lord of their lives, they would have to remove from their lives anything that was drawing them away from Him. This is not an easy decision and they needed to understand how difficult it would be. "You have to get rid of your friends that drag you to the bars and want to drink with you," I said. "You have to stop buying alcohol, period. If the TV makes you want to go buy beer, quit watching TV. Anything and everything that draws you away from God and is keeping you away from God, you have to remove from your life. Then you have to get in God's Word. His Word has to replace every bad habit you've ever had."

Richard said, "I want that. I'm ready for a change. I want to know God." But his wife said four very telling words that the devil had planted as an obstacle to the power of God's Word in her life. She said, "I have a book." She continued to tell me that this book was really helping her understand her life. In truth, Richard was serious about having a relationship with Jesus. His wife, on the other hand, was seeking to circumvent God's Word by following a popular author's secular view of God's word. Shortly after this conversation, she moved out of their home and began to patronize the bars daily. Richard became my disciple and joined a men's Bible study that met every Thursday morning. It was perfect timing on God's part for Richard's life. We were beginning a new study, the first of a four-part study that I had been writing for more than three years and that I had learned over more than 30 years.

At first glance, Richard is an unassuming and uncomplicated mechanic, much like the disciple Peter. The very basic things about the Christian life that we might assume a person who grows up in church knows and understands, Richard was hungry for, almost like a starving child. He was like a sponge. Everything we studied became a daily pursuit to the point that he would go home from work, sit down with his Bible, and literally fall asleep each night pursuing the truths within God's Word.

One of the first truths I learned most Christians are not taught in church, and many never truly understand, is our spiritual birth. Richard was no different. Richard had made a profession of faith but could not identify his own spiritual birth. In fact, he admitted to being utterly clueless to spiritual matters altogether. He often attended church worship out of the duty he learned as a child. The preaching was no more than babble and the music was more attractive than the preached word. It was as if he was attending church to be seen, participating in the singing part of worship, then turning the switch off and enduring the preaching part.

Something I learned early on about myself, and then about many of my fellow church members, is that I was taught that John 1:12 teaches I am a child of God because I received the gospel and believed in the name of Jesus. However, the significance of spiritual birth or when it takes place was never taught in an understandable manner. Over time, I have learned that an important first step to truly understanding salvation, spiritual life, and a personal relationship with God is to determine your personal spiritual birth; not necessarily when it took place, but whether there is actual evidence that it has taken place. Or as Jesus might say, "The wind blows. You don't know where it comes from or where it goes, but you will see evidence that it's windy." (Author's paraphrase; see John 3:8.)

How many times have you heard a preacher, nearing the end of the sermon, say, "You may have said a prayer sometime in your life but you can't identify a time or date." He might say, "Why not drive a stake in and nail it down today?" He might even say, "You're not truly saved if you can't identify the day and time." However, I have found that most Christians who can identify the exact day they said a prayer cannot even begin to describe spiritual birth as it applies to their own lives.

Most have never discussed the evidences of spiritual birth even though they have spent years in Sunday school or Bible studies learning moral rights and wrongs. I would even go as far as to say this is where churches have truly missed the mark in the area of making disciples. Most Christians will tell you they know the story of the important Jewish leader, Nicodemus, in John 3:1-21. He may have come to Jesus in the night earnestly seeking knowledge or he may have seen Jesus as someone who could give him an advantage over the ruling council. However, most Christians have very little understanding of Jesus' meaning in regard to how this story applies to their own beliefs of who Jesus is versus their own spiritual birth.

As I asked fellow church members and fellow Christian brothers and sisters to describe their spiritual birth, most simply said, "I don't know what you mean." Occasionally someone would say, "You can't explain that kind of thing. Even Jesus said you can't explain it." But when pressed for a description of the evidences of spiritual birth that they see in their own lives, many have no idea how to respond to that question.

As I see it, Jesus never even acknowledges Nicodemus' belief in Him as being from God. He simply points out that Nicodemus can't see the Kingdom of God because Jesus can't see any evidence of spiritual birth in Nicodemus. So, if we evaluate, say, a spiritual leader, and we write down everything we see that gives evidence of his spiritual birth, it might look something like this: An understanding of God's Word, a hunger to learn and teach others what he has learned in God's Word, a compassion for those for whom he truly has no responsibility, a kindness that causes him to go out of his way for others even in the middle of his night or day, a passion for others to know Jesus as their personal savior, a consistent prayer life that includes time alone with God daily, a realization of his spiritual dependency on God, and a genuine presence of God's Spirit that draws people to him.

Let's say we take those identifying evidences that we might see in a person who obviously has a spiritual life and apply them to ourselves. We would have to ask these questions: Do I have a love for God's Word? Do I understand and learn from it, maybe even have a desire to teach others because of what I've learned from it? Do I have a compassion for those in need but for whom I have no responsibility? Do I find myself being kind to others even when I'm busy? Do I see people in need of a savior and share the gospel of Jesus Christ? Do I have a consistent daily prayer life? Do I understand that I am spiritually dependent on God? Do others recognize God's Spirit in me?

When Richard was confronted with these spiritual evidences, they drew him to the conclusion that even though he had said a prayer when he was young and had been in church most of his life, he could not identify spiritual evidences in his own life, nor had he ever experienced someone else pointing out any evidences of spiritual birth in his life. He saw himself as a self-centered person with only a belief in God. Richard came to the conclusion that he was no longer satisfied with a simple religious belief and he wanted a personal relationship with Christ. It was at this point that he realized he needed to take the step that does cause spiritual birth to take place and place his faith in Jesus. He began to cry out to God for a spiritual birth.

Though Richard did not experience an identifiable emotional experience, what did happen is that God's Word began to come alive to Richard. He began to see himself in scripture and scripture began to speak directly to his life. Scriptures that he had grown up understanding as simply being Bible stories now became full of personal truths which brought questions to his mind that caused him to look deeper into God's Word. In short, he realized just how little of spiritual matters he had known and that he was utterly dependent on God for his spiritual life.

Other changes became evident as well. Richard began to see a need to help those around him who were suffering. He returned to his boyhood church where his mother was still a member. His former friendships that drew him away from God seemed to dissolve even without effort. He soon found himself compelled to support the church and God's kingdom work financially. His attitude, his conversation, even the way he approached everyday activities began to change before his eyes and the eyes of others. Richard's boss, his family, his co-workers, even parts-delivery people who came to the shop began to see a change in Richard. Those he was in Bible study with began to see a bright light come forth through his life. Soon his spiritual birth was not only evident, but it became the attractive, visible feature within his person and it was contagious.

It could be said, that without conscious effort, or intentional activity, spiritual birth came into Richard's life and the evidences increased day by day, kind of like a soft breeze rustling the leaves of a tree and increasing slowly to a howling, limb-bending wind. Many people who only knew Richard before his spiritual birth and hadn't been a part of the process saw him as having had a 180-degree conversion experience, kind of like walking out of a hot, windy West Texas day into a cool, air-conditioned living room. Nevertheless, his spiritual birth process was not instant. It did not happen overnight or even over a few days. In fact, if we asked Richard today, he would tell us it is not complete now, some four years later.

The huge difference in Richard's experience and that of many Christians is that Richard had disciple makers walking him through his spiritual birth. I personally had the privilege of opening God's Word almost daily with Richard. Often I saw evidence of his spiritual birth before he did and was blessed to point it out to him. I even had the privilege of teaching and discipling him using *The Carpenter's Four-Part Guide to Making Disciples (The Carpenter's Guide)* I had developed to help him become the true disciple maker he is today. Although Richard's spiritual birth was revealed gradually, it was no less powerful than the person who has a powerful conversion experience and a life-changing event that causes an about-face, repentant life change. His new birth affected many lives and I believe it would be fair to say his life has become a spring of living water.

One of the key turning points in Richard's life came during our study of John 3:1-21. In this passage of scripture, Nicodemus had heard what he needed in order to understand and believe all of scripture as well as who Jesus was and His purpose. However, Nic chose to accept logical, earthly understanding rather than placing his faith in the One he believed was from God. Jesus refused to even acknowledge who Nic understood Him to be. Jesus took what He knew Nic had learned in his Old Testament studies, and then described Himself as being like the healing snake pole Moses lifted for the Israelites; Nic could not accept this and failed to put his faith in Jesus. However, Richard saw he had to make a choice. He chose to place his faith in Jesus and not continue to rely on his belief of Jesus as merely a factual, historical person and important religious figure.

As the director of a mission ministry focused on teaching Christians to share their faith, I get to ask a lot of questions. Something I have learned from those questions is that a large portion of the Christian community walked the aisle of a church, prayed a prayer with the pastor or made a public profession of faith as a child or teen. For most, it was sincere and when the pastor said, "Because of your decision today you are eternally saved," they believed that made it a done deal. In other words, they had done their part and when they died they would go to heaven. I don't doubt or discount a single one of those decisions. However, when we ask them to describe how their life changed or whether they feel they were born again, the majority of them simply do not know how to answer. The most common answer I get is, "It doesn't work like that." When pressed to describe what happened or how they felt different, they give vague responses such as, "A peace came over me," "I simply felt my burdens lifted," or "It's hard for anyone to put that experience into words."

Again, I don't doubt that most understand exactly what they were doing and the purpose of questioning is not to cast doubt on anyone's salvation. Rather, it is to determine whether or not Christians understand their own spiritual birth. The fact is that most Christians have put their faith in Jesus, believing He died so that they could be forgiven of their sins, but few ever truly experience the spiritual life that Jesus has come to give. As disciple makers, we must teach other believers, whether they are new in their faith or long time church members, to see the evidence of spiritual birth in their day-to-day lives. We must stop saying, "If there were more to it, the preacher and teachers at my church would have taught us about it." Instead, we need to trust God's Word, and seek to understand that Jesus says, "Like the wind can't fully be explained, the spiritual birth cannot be fully explained. But if it's windy you better hold on to your hat and if you have the Spirit of God in you, the evidence, often called fruit, will change your life drastically and forever." (Author's paraphrase; see Galatians 5:22-23.)

The conflict of the spirit that Richard and many faithful church members face are not whether or not their salvation experience was real but, rather, whether the prayer of repentance they prayed as a child is all there is to being a true child of God. When someone is faced with this confusion, they first and foremost need a sound understanding of scripture. Without scriptural knowledge, it will be difficult at best to become a disciple of Jesus and impossible to become a disciple maker. Please don't twist what I'm saying. The American Christian way is to base our spiritual life on what the preacher says from the pulpit every Sunday morning. What I'm saying is, that's not enough! Scriptural knowledge comes from being in God's Word every day. It's also true that reading front to back through the Bible is a good thing, but to fully understand the spiritual life and gain the scriptural knowledge necessary to be a disciple maker, we must study, search, dwell and continually look at our lives compared to scripture in order to put our spiritual fruits to proper use.

Why is understanding spiritual birth the most important aspect of a full relationship with God? It is very simple. Jesus said to Nic, "unless one is born again he *cannot* see the kingdom of God." [Emphasis added.] This is clearly a here-and-now statement. Nicodemus, as well as many logical thinkers today, miss the kingdom all around us because of their death grip on who they believe God is and what they expect God to do in the lives of men. Nic had the preconceived belief that God's Messiah would conquer the Romans, and overpower all other kingdoms of the world, then re-empower the Jewish people. Today, many refuse to acknowledge God's Kingdom because the wealthy, the popular, and the powerful often see God as merely a crutch on which the less fortunate and less intelligent lean. Even in many Christians' lives, the belief that God is not concerned about their daily lives and is only interested in the big picture, an unexplained miracle, or the rapture and judgment is common. However, what I have learned, what Richard learned, and what every truly born-again believer learns is that God very much wants to be a part of our everyday lives.

When we are taught to see the difference in a born-again life and a life without God's Spirit in it, we can give evidence of our spiritual birth even if we can't fully explain how or when it occurred. As a disciple maker, I would tell you there are few greater joys in life than to see a grown man or woman lay his or her life down and to watch spiritual birth take place. When people like Richard begin to see God drawing people to him so the fruit of the Spirit can bless others, himself, and God, the joy is hard to put into words. When the Kingdom of God is a reality of our everyday life, God is no longer a mystical figure way up in heaven. No, he is a friend closer than a brother.

In addition, a humble power comes into our life that does not need to boast or to be put on a pedestal. When we come to recognize the evidences of spiritual birth, we no longer feel compelled to argue our doctrinal stance. Rather, we are consumed with developing spiritual fruit that gives greater evidence of the spiritual birth that has taken place in our lives. Our human ego is diminished by our enjoyment of producing Godly fruit, especially when this fruit is literally produced in and through our lives by the Holy Spirit of God that lives in us.

    I challenge every Christian reading this book to stop what you are doing, get out a pen and paper, and look in the mirror of your life. Write out a list of every evidence of spiritual birth, every evidence of spiritual fruit, and every life change that has taken place since you were born again. While you're at it, write down how you see God in your everyday life, how He uses you and draws others to you. Then write the names of three people whom you believe do not understand their own spiritual birth nor see the Kingdom of God as here and now. Just write them down. Don't stop reading because you think I'm going to ask you to do something you don't feel you can do. Just keep reading.

Chapter 2

Understanding the Relationship

"Because I live, you also will live. In that day you will know that I am in my Father, and you in me, and I in you." ~Jesus
(John 14:19b-21)

It is possible that **our position in our relationship with God** is the single-most misunderstood aspect of our Christian life. Our knowledge and understanding of our spiritual birth is what permits us to learn and grow a daily personal relationship with Christ. Most Christians have heard a lot of talk about having a relationship with Christ, but if we ask three people that we know are faithful church members to tell you what their relationship with Christ looks like, I promise we will not get more than a general answer that will sound something like this: "I pray every day and I know God hears my prayers, I read my Bible and He speaks to me through it, and when I go to church and worship it fills me up and I am blessed." These are all great benefits of the Christian life and they are truly evidences of a spiritual birth. But what happens if we ask that same person to tell us how their relationship with Christ differs or compares to their relationship with their spouse or parent, boyfriend or girlfriend, or maybe their best friend?

What will happen is this: We will learn just how few Christians can identify in detail what their personal relationship with Christ looks like? Over a three-year period, I asked this question to many Christians. Most were laymen, but several were preachers. I had a two-hour discussion with a seminary professor who teaches future pastors church relations and I learned that, in his words, it's impossible to describe a relationship with God because it is completely conducted on a spiritual plane not understandable to men on a basic human level. It took every ounce of self-control I had to not say, "HOG WASH!" We will get into that later. I had conversations with six career missionaries, two directors of family ministry, and four Baptist Sunday school directors in charge of putting together Bible study materials for their entire churches. Only a handful of those could give a confident answer and a real-life example from their own personal relationship with Christ.

Much like spiritual birth, the personal relationship with God is not well taught within most Christian churches. We most often hear of the relationship with Christ talked about within personal testimonies and usually just after a tremendous spiritual experience like a mission trip. As a matter of fact, it is so scarcely discussed among small group Bible studies that the average Christian would be at a complete loss if they were asked where in scripture it teaches a personal relationship with Christ. What we do find is that most Christians, though they have never shared their faith with a lost person, believe that every lost person needs to say a prayer of repentance and ask Jesus to be Lord of his or her life, and then they need to follow Jesus in baptism and become a member of the local church. Subsequently, a large portion of faithful church members can share every detail of how they were saved and what being a member of First Baptist Church looks like, but a relationship with Jesus is still a foreign concept to them.

As a student of Christ, I have learned that Jesus never assumed men could be taught a spiritual relationship. When I study His interactions with His disciples, it is obvious He has no expectations of them fully grasping this relationship through a single upper room lesson. Rather, He insists that they travel through life with Him. Even after living with Him for at least a year and a half, traveling alongside Him, and even participating in His miracles, they don't understand the relationship He has with His Father. They only see Him as one with the authority of God and a powerful knowledge of the Word of God.

Then perhaps the most important life lesson Jesus demonstrates to His disciples and to us takes place. They are in Capernaum during the census when every person over the age of 20 was required to pay a half-shekel offering as support for the tabernacle. Here we get a closer look at the age of the disciples. Jesus tells Peter to go fishing, catch a fish and take the shekel out the fish's mouth and pay His and

Peter's temple tax, giving us the impression that only He and Peter were over 20 years of age. (See Matthew 17:27.)

This event sets the stage for an argument among the disciples which eventually leads to them asking Jesus the million dollar question: "Who will be the greatest in the kingdom of heaven?" Is it Peter because he is older? Is it John whom Jesus loves? Who will be the greatest and how do they position themselves in the best position to become the greatest? This is human nature and its selfish understanding of relationships and how we can manipulate them to our advantage. In our human nature, there is always a pecking order and we start toward the top of it at birth by begging for our mother's attention. We don't even realize we are in this competition, but it consumes our early years of life and often we win Mom's total devotion and lose a loving relationship with Dad altogether.

How we grow up in church is not much different. I recall when my son was seven or eight; he loved to read and was a very fast reader as well. One day on the way home from church he said, "Mr. Bragg let me teach today, Dad." He went on to explain how he had read the lesson before class started and when Mr. Bragg asked if anyone knew what today's lesson was, he knew more than Mr. Bragg did, so he just told my son to teach it. Innocent enough, right? From then on my son was labeled by all the other children as a spiritual leader. This followed him all the way through high school, but when he left the youth group, stepped out into college where everybody is somebody, he was no longer a spiritual leader. In fact, his relationship with Christ began to struggle and it was not until the middle of law school, five or six years later that the evidence of a spiritual relationship became a key part of his life.

Why is it so important to understand how we grow up and mature as a Christian? Very simple. If we, as Christians, and more importantly as disciple makers, learn to lead and train our children how to grow up in a strong personal relationship with Christ, the disciple-making process will be catapulted into overdrive. The Church as a whole will once again have the primary goal of making disciples as its purpose, just as Christ commissioned it to have. This truth, though agreed with, will not be, and is not, popular in most churches in our society today. For the most part, church leaders are offended and feel somewhat threatened by a membership that is fully equipped to make disciples. I risk ruffling many feathers by making such a statement, but the facts support what I am saying and the expansion of the Gospel and the multiplication of disciples is at an all-time low everywhere except in a small area of the foreign mission field.

The current growth of the Kingdom of God in the U.S. alone is so far behind the population growth that in a few short years, Christians will be an extreme minority and the number of evangelical churches will fall like rocks off Mount Everest. This will not be because we didn't vote in the political election (something we should do at every opportunity). It will be because we do not practice making disciples of Christ and we do not know how to get started. Even the very basics, like a personal relationship with God, are misunderstood at best and seldom taught within the four walls of churches. Preachers do a great job of using God's Word to motivate people to live good lives, to be faithful, to attend church and tithe. They do a fair job of leading people to be obedient to the commands of Christ. Most church members can recite John 3:16 and explain what it means. But let's get real for a minute. Many Christian surveys show eight-out-of-ten professing Christians over the age of 18 have never shared the gospel or even their faith with one person. Please, someone, somewhere, in some pulpit, in some seminary class, in some prayer breakfast, youth camp or, for Pete's sake, in one of those pastors' conferences ask, or better yet, answer the question, "If Christianity in America is doing such a great job of fulfilling the great commission of Christ, why in the world are 80% of professing Christians are not prepared to share their faith, and even fewer are equipped to be obedient and make disciples?"

Here's my humble take on this matter. People share with others their relational experiences, both good and bad. We share about those we love and interact with every day. You don't have to ask a 25-year-old newlywed if he just got married because his wife is all he talks about. You don't have to ask a mother how her kids are doing more than once to hear their life stories. You don't have to ask a grandparent anything, because before you can say "hello," they are showing the photos and telling you the silly thing their grandbabies did. You don't have to ask a teenage girl if she has a boyfriend because she probably has it posted on

Facebook every minute of every day since the guy winked at her in math class. However, 80 percent of professing Christians have never talked about Jesus with even one lost person and most are afraid they will offend someone in the restaurant if they pray too loudly before eating because the other patrons don't know Jesus. That 80 percent know exactly who Jesus is and most have the fish on the bumper of their car and a closet full of Christian t-shirts to prove it, but start a conversation with them about what Jesus did in their lives this week and they will scatter like a covey of quail with a bird dog around.

So let's get to where I'm going with this. The second basic understanding that a disciple of Christ must have is that of his personal relationship with Christ. Even though I had realized Christ had chosen me to be his disciple, I had no idea where to go with it except to my knees. I counseled with my pastor who told me I was in the brotherhood ministry and that was the best place to learn. I was skeptical because I had been serving in the men's ministry for a couple of years and the thing I felt was its biggest priority was the church-league softball team. It was great fun and some of those men became good friends, but I was never challenged spiritually and my understanding of my relationship with Christ did not grow.

What did happen was that we began to go on mission serving needy people in our city and the border area of South Texas. One of the first times I encountered Christ in such a way that I knew He had drawn me to the place and the very moment to show me He was my personal Lord was in 1980. I was in a small Mexican border town called Piedras Negras. We were there to build a small block church house beside the Rio Grande River. When we arrived, only the back wall of the building made of cement blocks was about two-thirds complete. It was our task to complete the structure which started with mixing a huge amount of cement by hand on the ground.

One morning, just after the fog lifted, I heard the sound of a baby crying. I peered over the wall and directly behind the church was a very small adobe house. It looked like it was about the size of a one-car garage. There was a burlap sack fashioned as a door and a young woman, who was holding a bucket in one hand and the door back with the other hand, was hollering at children to get outside. One by one I watched and counted as 14 children and three more grown women exited the house. The kids, from barely walking to around 12 years old, scattered to who knows where and the four ladies went to work on that little house.

They carried five-gallon buckets of water up and down the steep river bank and, with the water and a straw broom; they cleaned and swept every inch of that house. God's Spirit compelled me to get a closer look so, at the risk of making my teammates mad by stealing their lunch snack; I took a case of Hostess cupcakes over and offered them as a gift. The house had a dirt floor, dampened and packed hard by use, and the only visible furnishing I saw was a makeshift table. One of the ladies was rolling tortilla dough in a pool of flour on the table. As I handed those women some gospel tracts and turned to walk away, I heard the verse of scripture in Luke 19 when Jesus looked on the perishing city of Bethany and, full of compassion, wept at their pending plight. My spirit, my heart hurt and I realized that I was feeling what Jesus felt on that day looking over a hell-bound people.

It was in that very moment that I realized Jesus was showing Himself to me in real time, in a real way that I could relate to in my humanity. He allowed me to feel and even see what He saw. He saw more coming out of that house than a bunch of dirty-faced kids and hard-working women. It was His creation and they were headed for eternal damnation. What I really wish I could say is that in that very moment, I saw my relationship with Jesus. The truth is, however, at the time, my relationship with Jesus was a fleeting thought. No one else on my team saw or experienced this and no one said to me, "This is how Jesus lets us be a part of His life." No one said, "You now know how Jesus feels when we walk away from His creation without sharing the truth of the Gospel." In that moment, I needed a disciple maker even if for a moment to look me in the eye and tell me that I had just encountered Jesus.

Jesus walked hand-in-hand with His disciples and much of what He talked about, much of what He demonstrated daily, much of what He taught that actually stuck with them was about the relationship with God that is available to every child of God. So if we are teaching another about the relationship Jesus demonstrates in scripture, it's important to focus on what Jesus put emphasis on. In John 14 in particular, we see how utterly dependent

Jesus was on His Father. For us to have a right relationship with God, we also must humble ourselves to a point of complete dependence on God. In John 14:24, Jesus even says the words He speaks are not His own but the Father's. This dependence created a oneness so powerful that Jesus literally pointed out that if we keep His commands and follow His words and are as dependent on Him as He is on the Father, we can know that same oneness with God.

How do we humble ourselves and, better yet, how do we teach this to others? The answer is Jesus! He demonstrated how in terms that everyone listening can understand. In Matthew 18, when Jesus' disciples were in an argument over what will make one have greater position in the Kingdom of Heaven over the others, Jesus simply demonstrated it in such a way that no one questioned Him. He brought to Himself what I believe was a toddler who was just barely walking and in need of a parent to hold his hands in order to even stabilize his body. In other words, the child was completely dependent on Jesus to help him stand or walk. However, much like all of us, the disciples viewed themselves in one way or another as being superior to the others. Peter might have said, "I'm the oldest," while John argued that he was the one closest to Jesus. Andrew probably said, "I was the first to notice Jesus was the Messiah." These are all very proud, adult arguments.

What Jesus demonstrated, and even said, was that unless the disciples, and we, turn from our attitudes of adultness and realize that God is our spiritual Father and we are forever His children, we can never even enter the

Kingdom of Heaven. As humans, we tend to view all things according to what we understand in our physical lives. We have virtually no understanding of spiritual matters at all. This is especially true with regard to how we pray, or communicate, with God. Most of the time we approach God in prayer like grownups who have earned the right to have a sit-down-and-talk conversation with God. Even when we try to humble ourselves, it is limited to how we approach God, but we still quickly get to our requests, our childlike dependence disappears, and we begin to ask for things like God is a rich relative rather than a loving Father who sees what we need and ignores what we want.

    What Jesus demonstrated to His disciples that day was a child who was so dependent that without Jesus' help he couldn't even stand. When we study this, we see that the child was so small, so dependent that he couldn't ask for anything. The truth is that the child didn't have to, because Jesus responded to the need of the child and the child simply depended on Him. If we want a real relationship with Jesus, this is where we start. We cannot come to God as an adult full of knowledge and wisdom. We cannot even come to God as old enough to beg for what we want. I'm not saying that God will not hear us. I am saying that Jesus never says or teaches that if we ask in a certain way He will hear and give us what we want. When we are completely dependent on God, He sees and knows our needs before we ever ask and our asking soon becomes a result of our faith that He already knows what is needed. When we are completely dependent on God, we accept whatever His answer is and take another step because He is there to meet our needs.

As we mature and grow in spiritual experience, we find that a greater dependence on God for understanding develops. We begin to experience Jesus not through begging for a revelation but through an awareness of Him in our everyday activities. He reveals Himself spiritually in such a way that we can see things from His point of view, we can feel His heartaches and joys, and we can know He is present in the way He uses our physical experiences to reveal how personal our relationship with Him really is.

As adults, we tend to take things for granted. For instance, we believe that when we grow up, get married, and pay our own bills, mom and dad should no longer look at us like little kids but like equals. However, it's not until we become parents of grown children ourselves do we realize that, to parents, children are always kids. Likewise, to a perfect God who knows all things, we are always children completely dependent on Him for every spiritual understanding.

Unfortunately, in today's society, Christian growth is for the most part dictated by church attendance. We should never discourage anyone from being faithful to church nor should we discount the effect that good, sound preaching has on our spiritual lives. But if we limit the growth of our relationship with God to once or twice a week, we will find ourselves much like a baby who gets one or two good bottles of milk a week suffering from malnutrition. Having a right relationship with Christ on a daily basis will lead to a greater corporate worship experience and cause greater growth in our spiritual lives as well. When our personal relationship with God is daily, we in turn build up the Church and we mobilize ourselves and other followers of Christ to be about the work of making disciples.

When Jesus is our example, disciple makers begin to teach others to understand the relationship with God by walking through life's experiences with them and helping them see and understand how God is drawing them and showing Himself to them in very real and very personal ways. For example, I was walking alongside a younger disciple named Travis. He had a child with Down's Syndrome and God was calling him to interact with a home for disabled people in Mexico. We had gone through the facility and heard the incredible story of how God had raised it up and how it was meeting the needs of many abandoned and forgotten physically and mentally disabled patients. We were about to exit when a young lady about 20 years old with Down's Syndrome walked in. She came to the first person in line and shook his hand, smiled and moved to the next. She shook my hand but never looked at me. Travis was next and when she took his hand, she immediately looked up at this six-foot-eight giant and smiled, and then she reached out and wrapped her arms around him and hugged him tight. With tears in his eyes, he exited that place. I had the privilege of saying, "Travis, whether you realize it or not, Jesus just gave you a hug." Thankfully, he understood and saw how Jesus had drawn him there for that very moment that he might interact with Him in a way that was personal to Travis alone.

Most Christians miss this kind of interaction with Christ, not because of churches or preachers, but because there are simply very few disciple makers that see the need to help other believers see their relationship with Christ in real time. We should never see age or length of church membership as being a precedent for maturity or spiritual growth.

In scripture, we see that a key component of a mature disciple is being filled with the Spirit. In Acts 6:3, even the basic servants were chosen based on one primary characteristic: They were known to be full of the Spirit. We never see Jesus choose to have a relationship with a person, for example His disciples, based on their age or wisdom. I believe when we take a look at how He chose His disciples, it becomes clear that He chose those willing to have a relationship with Him. Jesus did not just walk down a road one day, see Simon (Peter), say, "Come, follow me," and Peter jumped up and tagged along. I will challenge you to pose a question to as many Christians as you are willing to. Ask your Sunday school or Bible study class, a close friend, and family members and discover what they believe about how Jesus called His disciples. I began several years ago to ask my Christian friends, "How did Jesus call His disciples?" I found out that more than 90% had never studied all four gospel accounts of Jesus calling His disciples. Subsequently, the majority believed Jesus had never seen any of the disciples before and simply walked up to strangers, said, "Come, follow me," and they jumped up and, like dogs on a leash, they followed. No, the truth is that Jesus' ministry was in full swing. He came into their workplace and performed a miracle and it so impacted their lives that it caused them to say, "I want a relationship with this guy." (See Luke 5:1-11.)

When we are disciple makers, we don't just expect others to follow us because we have the Spirit of God in our hearts and knowledge of how to experience more from the Christian life than great worship one day a week. The truth is that when we are prepared to make disciples, God will draw someone into our lives so that He might make us His disciple maker. In other words, He will use our relationship with Him to draw another to us that He might reveal the relationship He wants with that person. That is a mind twister, but it's the truth. I have come to learn that if we try to force or ask another to be a disciple, they may commit to meet with us and even be very sincere but, in my personal experience, they very seldom will follow through and become a disciple of Jesus. I am not saying we shouldn't ask others to be disciples. What I am saying is, if we think we are going to take an insurance salesman's approach and start cold calling others to be disciples, we are going to be very frustrated individuals.

This one truth alone will revolutionize the spiritual life of many of the 80 percent of Christians who have never shared their faith even once. Look at it this way: If some stranger, or even someone we go to church with, walks up to us and says, "Come walk this 50-mile stretch of rough treacherous road with me, there could be a pot of gold at the end of it," how apt are we to say, "Sure I'll go with you?" But what if the same guy walks past us carrying a chunk of gold and says, "If you want some, you have to travel a treacherous 50-mile road with me, but the rewards are great." How much more apt are we to not just be willing but actually *wanting* to go? What I am saying is this: When Jesus is our best friend, we can't hide it. Those who are searching for a greater relationship with Jesus will be drawn to us not because of what might be, but because they want what they know we already have.

As disciple makers, we have the responsibility to follow Jesus' example. Jesus' life and actions are our example of how everything in God's kingdom functions. For us to properly lead another into a right relationship with Jesus, we must take a long look at how He interacts with the Father. In every situation of Jesus' life, we see Him talking and interacting with the Father first, then He acts accordingly, in obedience to the Father's directions. In short, Jesus' example is to simply and utterly be obedient to the Father.

In our adultness, we often forget who we are talking to in prayer. We forget that God is not a man and God will not be addressed as a man. When we, in our adultness, forget to place God in the proper position of Father and we come to Him with an attitude of anything other than an obedient child, God's ears will turn deaf to our self-centered prayers. Often, when we start gaining scriptural knowledge and wisdom, we see ourselves as more Christ-like than our fellow Christians. We then attempt to pray in this attitude of superiority and God the Father is not impressed at all. He then will draw our attention to the completely dependent little child and we will be put in our place. In our stubbornness, we reject our true need and start acting and making decisions that affect many lives, sometimes entire congregations, in our own power and adult maturity just to find we are not in control after all. Things we lead begin to go wildly wrong and we come to realize God is not in it.

A child never takes control. We must realize that God the Father knows our every spiritual, physical, and emotional need and if we simply love the Father and accept Him as being in charge, things will turn out for the best. The key we must convey to all disciples is that our relationship with God only works if we are children utterly in need of the Father's direction, the Father's wisdom and, most importantly, the Father's love. So the second critical truth every disciple must understand and accept is that **God is always the Father in the relationship and we are always the child.**

When we fully understand and see our spiritual birth and trust in the evidence as it is identified by scripture and confirmed by other believers, we can begin to accept our position as a fully dependent child in our relationship with God. The frustration of growing in knowledge but feeling more dependent spiritually on God will disappear. We will begin to find joy in everyday experiences, because we will see God in every part of our lives. Before we reach this point, it's hard to fully trust God and live like His child rather than seek to live life the popular way.

Chapter 3

A Child of God

*"**T**ruly, I say to you, whoever does not receive the kingdom of God like a child shall not enter it."*
~Jesus
(Mark 10:15)

Living this life like a child of God must be intentional. I have come to believe that living every day like a child of God is the single-most challenging aspect of a disciple's life and a part of the Christian life that few fully experience. I have also learned that living as a child of God daily is impossible without the Holy Spirit guiding our lives. We can fool the world on Sunday morning, but is the world so foolish on Friday night? What I mean is this: When we go out to the Friday night football game, a favorite restaurant, or maybe a movie, do our attitudes, choices and actions reflect to others that we are children of God, or are we simply doing what everyone else does because it's fun, enjoyable, and our way of life? Again, don't twist what I am saying. I am not saying we shouldn't eat out in the popular restaurant or go to the football game and the movies. I am saying when we go out for entertainment or pleasure, we should put on the full armor of God and prepare to be different than those who claim to be Christians but leave their spiritual lives at the door of the church.

For disciple makers, it is imperative that we know the difference and teach others not to ignore that still, soft voice that speaks to our spirit and causes us to see how to reflect Christ even at a losing football game. My friend and disciple, Richard, had to set boundaries that helped him train himself to depend on the Holy Spirit. He stopped going anywhere that he might be known as a drinker or a partier. He disconnected the TV cable and stopped watching programs that train so many Christians to be tolerant of a sinful lifestyles. He started joining Bible studies and surrounding himself with Godly people who reflected Christ and the life of a child of God. He learned first what it meant to be a child of God, what excites children of God, and how children of God stand out and differ from those who do not follow Christ *before* he went into the community at large and attempted to do what is not natural. In other words, he first became comfortable with himself as a child of God.

Richard had studied the parables, paying special attention to those just after Jesus' disciples had chosen to follow Him. The one that spoke to him at this point in his life was the parable of the wine skins. When Jesus describes how the new and old skins cannot be sown together, Richard understood that to mean he could not be a child of God and act like he had in the past. Jesus used this verse to reveal to Richard that a complete change of life was necessary for him to ever overcome his past life and the desire to go along to get along. Scripture must be our guide as we disciple. As a result, God's Word will confirm what we teach and speak directly into each individual's life regardless of what their past life without Christ may have looked like.

One day while in a Bible study in Romans 8, we were asked to define the law of sin. After much debate, the consensus emerged that the law of sin was an unwritten law whereby sin has control or authority over our decisions, our actions, and our lives. It's incredible how few of us are willing to admit sin has any control over our lives! Nevertheless, I challenged the group to face sin and write down at least three sins they felt influenced the way they live. It might be a surprise to learn the sin that was on every single one of our lists. No, it was not lust, although it was on the list. Everyone in the group listed watching secular television as a sin that influenced their life decisions and subconsciously controlled their lives.

The point is, though most Christians do not view something as innocent as watching TV as a sin. But when we look at the effect watching TV has on our decision making, our tolerance and our view of God, we will realize it has sinful effects on our lives. As disciple makers, we must lead others to understand that everything we allow into our minds of a sinful nature leads to sinful choices and will ultimately cause us to view our relationship with God with a secular world view rather than a Godly, spiritual view.

These small, seemingly insignificant influences that corrupt our right reflection of Christ are the exact things that the armor of God described in Ephesians 6 is intended to help us fight against and defeat.

We are born with a sinful nature, one that we will have to overcome if we are to reflect the goodness of God on lost and sin-controlled people. Defeating our nature is no simple or easy task. However, when we begin to focus on making righteous, godly choices in our everyday, small, somewhat insignificant choices, our whole life begins to reflect on God our Father.

My good friend and prayer partner, Mike, used to tell his teenage son that his last name was Hymer and every choice he would make while out with his friends late at night would reflect on his father and the good name Hymer in the morning. I learned early on that when I, as a disciple, make choices based on how people who don't have a relationship with Christ might respond to my choices and decisions, I ultimately lose the ability to reflect the positive love of God, and the effect it has had on my life, onto their lives. Understanding what living like a child of God really looks like and how the little, everyday choices we make reflect on our Lord is crucial to the process of making disciples.

We must also face the fact that our nature is sinful and without the Spirit of God that comes into our lives at the point of spiritual birth, we cannot make good, righteous choices that reflect to others that we are children and disciples of the Most High God. This sounds really hard, but the truth is, if we learn to trust the Spirit of God in us, we will make those righteous choices and we will reflect the love of God on the lives of those around us. I had to learn that God does not strike us down with a lightning bolt and all of a sudden we automatically begin to make only right choices. It's a process.

Once we understand that God never forces us to make Godly choices, we can then begin to realize that by God allowing us to make bad choices He helps us understand how to make good choices. As we make good choices, we soon begin to understand how they reflect on God. We start to understand how those choices bring us closer to God and we learn just how much our righteous choices please God. When we are born again and God places His Spirit in us, we are as much His child as Jesus is His Son and we are aware of the choices that reflect positively and negatively on God. Once God places His Spirit in you, it is impossible to no longer be a child of God. Just like it's impossible not to be our earthly, biological father's child, it's impossible to take the Spirit of God out of our lives and no longer be children of God, even for the one who intentionally tries to no longer be a child of God.

Jesus makes this perfectly clear in John 8:31-36 when He announces to the Pharisees that those who have chosen to put their faith in Him would know the difference in living under the control of sin and living as children of God. Ultimately, living as children of God and making righteous choices will set them completely free from sin's control over their lives. However, if we want sin, we can have it. All we have to do is dwell on sin and we will eventually try sin. Sin will then have us in its grip and soon it will control our hearts and minds and the peace of God will no longer free us from sin's prison.

Many men and women today have experienced salvation and put their faith in Christ and the Gospel. Most are convinced that accepting God's salvation makes them disciples. However, the truth is that very few have entered into a disciple's relationship with Christ. Subsequently, our churches are full of believers that grow slower than an oak tree and weaker than a tumbleweed. Their entire understanding of Christ is formed from a 30 to 45-minute service on Sunday morning. The real tragedy in this is that many church leaders are satisfied with full pews regardless of whether lives are changed or not and most Christians are satisfied with doing their duty and showing up at church to be counted once a week.

What really defines a disciple? Is it that they attend church every time the door is open? Maybe it's that they can quote scripture right and left. It could be that they are the Christians whom everyone thinks of as spiritual. A sure-fire way to find out is ask them. What? Just ask them if they are a disciple or just a good saved Christian. That very simple question changed the course of my life. God used that question to draw me into a disciple's relationship and set my feet on a path that was covered with the footprints of Jesus.

The first thing God did to draw me into a disciple's relationship was to **take me out of my comfort zone and teach me just how little of Him was in my life**. The truth was I was a good Christian with all the right values and moral practices. I seldom missed a Sunday service and served all over the church, but I had no individual experience with God. I read the Bible through and could hold my own any time a Bible trivia game started. Yet at the same time, I could not give even one experiential example of my relationship with Christ. In fact, when I was asked if I was a disciple, I began to throw out the pat, good ole boy, response of "I don't know about that but the only difference in me and every other sinner in this old world is that I'm a saved sinner and they are just sinners."

Sound familiar? Never once did I ever have a single Christian tell me how bad the saved-sinner theology was. No, I had to learn it the hard, tedious way. That was until an older disciple challenged me to take a long look at my life compared to Jesus alone. I was in my late thirties now and I thought I had come along way. I had begun to see myself as a disciple rather than a saved sinner. However, this was the first time in my Christian life that an older Christian brother had ever shown an interest in my spiritual life with Christ. His name was Howard Kessler and he was in his seventies. He had been a part of the Navigator's (a ministry dedicated to making disciples) for many years.

Howard was only in my life for a few months but my spiritual growth jumped leaps and bounds in that short time. I learned two major truths that define the life of a disciple. The first truth is that **disciples are not satisfied with simply reading God's Word.** They find it necessary to study and dig in it until it literally comes to life for them.

The living scriptures are then memorized and they fill us with a passion for sharing God's Word with others.

The second truth is that **God's incredible love magnifies the relationship** He (the Father) wants with us (the child). In turn, we are filled with an undeniable love for God, for our Lord Jesus and all His children. Jesus is *our* example just as His life on earth was for His disciples. Jesus loved humanity so much that He laid down His glory and perfect heavenly life to extend His forgiveness to us. He loved us so much that though He was sinless, He took all our sins upon Himself and died a sinner's death so that we might be saved through His one act of righteousness. He demonstrated His command in John 15:1-17 and laid down His glory-filled life for us. Only when we truly have a disciple's love for our Lord and God will we ever lay down our lives and love sinners to salvation. Only through our love for God will we ever be able to see His love for His children.

As a disciple of Christ, my relationship with Jesus comes first and is more valuable to me than my own life. When those who have been born of the Spirit into God's family see another family member (Christian) with a great relationship with Christ, they are drawn to that person the same way the leper, the paralyzed, and the bleeding woman were drawn to Jesus for His healing touch. When we, as disciple makers, are able to live our relationship openly and without fear, others who want more out of the Christian life than duty and routine are drawn to see what it is that we have and it is at that point the disciple-making process begins.

PART 2

The Constitution of Righteousness

"Everyone then who hears these words of mine and does them will be like a wise man who built his house on the rock." ~*Jesus*
(Matthew 7:24)

Chapter 4

The Blessed Attitudes

"Blessed are the poor in spirit, for theirs is the kingdom of heaven."
~Jesus
(Matthew 5:3)

    A few years ago, God placed a man just a few years older than I in my life who had a strong desire to be a disciple. His name was John and he worked for me as a carpenter, so I had direct contact with him every day. John was a very intelligent man but had no formal education to speak of. He was one of those guys who read his Bible daily and was faithful to his local church but had no discipline when it came to studying God's Word or following an organized lesson manual. He needed someone to challenge him to look at his relationship with Christ every day until he realized what was lacking in his efforts to be a disciple of Christ. John understood his spiritual birth, he had a great deal of humility, and it was evident his relationship with Christ was good.

I remember the day I asked John to explain the first beatitude: Mathew 5:3. **"Blessed are the poor in spirit, for theirs is the kingdom of heaven."** He immediately said, "The real humble folks will surely go to heaven." He added, "You don't get much more humble than me and mine." John really was a humble guy and the truth is many Christians misunderstand this verse. To John, poor equaled humility while arrogance and pride equaled wealth, status and success. And to a great degree he is right. But I pushed John to look a little deeper at this verse by asking him, "What does a truly poor person need?" He saw himself as poor, but in truth John was self-sufficient for all his necessities. After a hard look at himself, John answered, "A poor person needs everything."

When Jesus said, "Blessed are the poor in spirit," He was literally saying blessed is the one who realizes he has nothing to contribute spiritually to God and that he is utterly and completely dependent on God. In other words, the person that recognizes God does not want or need him to be spiritual and turns to God for all things spiritual, be it big or small, has exactly what it takes, the basic requirement, to live and thrive in the Kingdom of Heaven.

There is something bigger going on here and it brings up an even deeper question. Does the fact that Jesus puts this beatitude first in His lesson on righteousness give it a higher place of importance in the overall teaching? I believe there is nothing chaotic or random about anything Jesus did. He very intentionally places choosing to recognize our spiritual position as complete dependence on

God first because the only way to ever realize a life conformed to this constitution of righteousness is to completely rely upon God. As John and I studied and casually discussed this vital teaching, we soon realized that for us, as sinful men, to even begin to develop a righteous life, we would first have to learn to run back to this very first, necessary position and fall on our faces before God and beg for His help and spiritual wisdom.

"Blessed are those who mourn, for they shall be comforted." (Matthew 5:4) The second beatitude holds a very high place in the order of having a right relationship with Christ or, in other words, a righteous person's attitude, because it speaks to our choice to view a lost person the same way Jesus did as He walked through the hell-bound crowds of people here on earth. (See Matthew 9:35-38.) As a youth, I went to a very small church out in West Texas. The pastor was going to seminary so I took everything he preached as the literal truth. When a girl in my school died in a car wreck, he preached her funeral. He used "blessed are those who mourn" as the comforting text of his sermon and I understood that to be the meaning of this passage. Unfortunately, like many Christians, I simply accepted this as mourning for a friend or loved one who has died and that one day God will wipe away our tears.

After I became a disciple in training, I learned what Jesus really meant by mourn, but I really had no experience with compassion for the lost to help me fully relate to how deeply Jesus mourned for those headed to hell. That was until I went on mission to specifically share the gospel with lost people. I led over 20 men to pray and accept Jesus as Lord of their lives. When I returned home, I was different. I could not keep from sharing the gospel with those I encountered. A young guy named Ricky worked for me at the time. He had lost his driver's license due to a DUI charge. Ricky and his mother lived next door to me and I took him to work and brought him home every day.

One day shortly after my return from mission, I was headed home with Ricky and he asked me if Christian music was all I ever listened to. That question opened the door for me to share my story and the Gospel with him. As I talked, I was amazed at how clearly I was able to present the Word of God to him. Most of the Gospel he had already heard, and even finished many of the verses that I was quoting. Before I got to the big question, I was pretty sure I was talking to a Christian. However, when I asked Ricky if he had ever made Jesus Lord of his life, he quickly said, "No, I have heard all that religious stuff and I believe in Jesus but I'm not ready to give up partying and having fun. Maybe I will someday." I spent the next half hour trying to help him understand what rejecting God's gift meant if he died before he "was ready." In the end, he simply said, "I know everything you are saying is probably true but I don't want it; Period!"

As Ricky got out of my truck and walked away, my heart broke. Maybe for the first time in my life, I had witnessed a person who knew exactly who Jesus was and what the gift of eternal life really looked like and rejected it anyway. I was literally sick to my stomach. I began mourning for this young man who the next morning was headed to jail for 14 months. I truly understood for the first time what Jesus meant in Matthew 5:4: "Blessed are those who mourn." But that was not the end.

It took me a couple of days to get my head around why I could go to a foreign country and lead several men, most of whom had never heard the Gospel before, to give their lives to Christ and come home and see complete rejection of the love of God right in my own driveway. To be honest, I just had no idea that there were people who could be so hard as to reject God's gift of love and sacrifice to save them from eternal damnation. I remember begging God to help me understand how Ricky could fully know and yet reject Jesus. I wish I could say God gave me an immediate answer, but the truth is I still don't fully understand. What God did next, though, was to give me a clear understanding of the whole meaning of Matthew 5:4.

A couple of days later, I was going to visit a friend I had not seen in a while. His house sat on a busy street with a lot of road noise. He also had a long driveway. I parked near the street and walked up to his door. Just before I rang the doorbell, I heard someone call my name. I turned to see a man walking up the drive toward me. At first I didn't recognize, him but it was obvious he knew me. He was dressed in a security guard's uniform and looked like a sharp, clean-cut man. As he got closer, I realized he was a man that I had shared the gospel with six years earlier. His name was Kevin and six years earlier he was at least a hundred pounds heavier, had long, dirty, stringy hair, and had a very hard time putting down his beer long enough to hear about God's gift.

Instantly, the conversation we had six years earlier came to my mind. Kevin understood the Gospel but he simply could not accept that God wanted him just like he was. I remember him telling me that his mother would not even hug him and he was not about to walk the aisle of a church looking like some white trash hoodlum. He didn't flat out reject the gospel. He wanted it, but he just couldn't believe that God would accept him just like he was. I will tell you, at the time, I felt he just wasn't ready to give up his La-Z-Boy recliner and beer cooler.

Standing in that driveway, I looked him up and down as he shared how he had cleaned his life up, how he know had a good job, and how he had stopped drinking all day. For several minutes he told me all about his new life and appearance, but he never mentioned God once. When he paused, I asked him, "Kevin, I can see you have changed and you look great. Your life is obviously cleaned up and better. But let me ask you this: What have you done with God's gift and your eternal destination?" His head dropped and he said, "I haven't done anything about it, but I have really been thinking about that a lot lately." My friend came out of his house about that time and another person came up and the opportunity to talk with Kevin disappeared. But the Holy Spirit would not let me leave it alone. During our conversation, Kevin had told me that he was working nights and slept until three in the afternoon.

All that night I prayed for Kevin. I knew he was under great conviction. The next day I was like a long-tailed cat in a room full of rocking chairs. I couldn't wait until three p.m. rolled around. At exactly three o'clock, I knocked on Kevin's door. He still lived in the same house he had lived in six years earlier. With my sharp sword (Bible) in hand, I greeted Kevin. He had a smile on his face and said, "Tell me how to get right with God." I went back through the Gospel step-by-step with him and this time he recorded every word. Kevin stopped me at Romans 10:13 and said, "That's what I need to do now, right"

Kevin prayed a prayer of repentance and begged God to come into his life, be his Lord, and save him. There on that front porch, Kevin got right all on his own. I was merely a witness to the fact. When I lifted my head, Kevin was leaned back against the wall and he said, "Glen, I feel like the whole weight of the world has just been lifted off my shoulders." He added, "I am finally free." He went on to tell me how the thought of rejecting God's gift had kept him awake many nights over the past few years. He wanted to be right with God but really didn't know who to ask. When he approached me the day before, it was for the sole purpose of hearing how to get right with God.

I left that porch, drove around the corner, stopped, and cried like a little girl who had just received the gift she had always wanted. After a good cry of thankfulness to God, I prayed, "Lord don't let Ricky forget, don't stop knocking on his heart, don't stop sending your disciples into his life." I wish at the time someone could have said to me that I had just experienced what Jesus wants every disciple to understand about Matthew 5:4. But it would be years before I understood all that my great Lord was doing that day.

"Blessed are the meek, for they shall inherit the earth." (Matthew 5:5) I believe this may be the most misunderstood of all the beatitudes, mostly because it is so hard to decipher between intentional action and personality. What I mean is that some people have a non-confrontational personality that causes them to avoid or run away from any potential conflict. When these people get into an argument, they clam up and tuck tail very quickly. Sometimes they are viewed as meek when, in truth, they are downright afraid of being involved in a potential conflict.

Another personality trait that is confused with meekness is timidity. I know a number of Christians who for one reason or another are so timid they are missing the blessing of experiencing God's powerful work because they are stuck in their comfortable safety zones. They don't share their faith and they seldom venture out to look for God at work or anywhere other than the safety of the church house. Some of these folks have a bubbly outgoing personality when at church or in their homes but become entirely different people outside in the general community. Because of this, they are more often viewed as meek rather than scared or timid. In Second Timothy 1:7, it is made very clear that a spirit of fear and timidity does not come from God. So when fear and timidity enter our lives, we should challenge it in the name of Jesus. We should never permit it to control or even let it influence our decision-making process at all.

My father-in-law was a meek man, but it was not until his death that I fully understood his true meekness. I was called on to preach his funeral message. I knew many things about him, having been around him for more than 30 years or so. I knew he seldom if ever told anyone no. I knew he was always the first to help someone in need and I knew he had to be forced into a conflict. In preparing for his funeral, I learned much more about what made him so meek. It wasn't a personality trait, it wasn't his way. Rather, it was his choice. He had been drafted into World War II and was attached to an army infantry unit as a machine gunner. He was deployed out of Abilene, Texas with 692 other soldiers of which only seven returned alive. He was awarded the bronze star, together with five recorded accounts for bravery beyond the call of duty. He survived and fought again after having both legs severely injured and frost bitten up to his waist. He received two purple hearts for his injuries. He was not timid by any meaning of the word, but he chose not to force his will on others. In fact, his courageous service record was completely unknown to his extended family.

Even though I viewed my father-in-law as a meek man, the greatest example of Godly meekness I have found was in the founding director of the ministry I now direct, CrossVision International Missions, and my mentor, Joe Ed Lively. Joe was the first man I really knew who had a great and powerful relationship with Jesus. I first served on mission with Joe in 1995. He taught me more about being a disciple and focusing on having a relationship with Christ Jesus on that one mission than I had learned during the previous 15 years of going on mission and doing good works for God.

Joe was a man's man. He was an incredible athlete, a former Golden Glove boxer, held a black belt in judo, and had been an All-American high school football player. Joe was tough, strong and unwavering in his conviction and devotion to God. But more than that, this big, muscular, intimidating man was the epitome of Godly humility and meekness. Whether he was surrounded by angry Guatemalans or on his knees talking to a child, Joe was always as calm and patient as Jesus. The one time I saw him get upset enough to strike out, he stopped himself and said to the irate man, "I must go, but please take this matter to God and ask for His wisdom."

Joe never bragged of his meekness or explained why he was meek. He lived it on a daily basis and when he came up against something that contradicted his convictions and beliefs, he firmly stood his ground and sought to compassionately explain his stance with a genuine desire not to hurt another's feelings. In reality, Joe had grown up in a difficult situation with poor parents and nine brothers and sisters. He had to be tough and fight hard just to get a word in and be heard. Despite a lack of family support, he became an athletic force to be reckoned with. Joe didn't learn humility and meekness from family when he was young. He became meek once Jesus came into his life and changed his selfish desires.

When he learned he had a devastating, more-than-likely life-ending cancer, he fought to live and serve the Lord every day. He could have died any way he chose, but he had become a humble, meek bondservant of God. Even his death in 2001 was an obvious submission to God's will. The last words I ever heard Joe utter were, "I just want to serve Jesus." Only a truly Christ-like, meek man can ever grasp the humility and meekness it took for Jesus to be crucified by sinful men. It took me years after Joe's death to completely understand why he died such a hard death. But today I know his meekness and submission to God's will has led to a position of authority in the Kingdom of Heaven.

Blessed are those who hunger and thirst for righteousness, for they shall be satisfied." (Matthew 5:6) The person that hungers for righteousness (a right relationship with God) works and desires to see society and the normal tolerance of sin changed to a righteous norm. In other words, their passion, what drives them to serve the Lord, and the way they are satisfied is to actively perpetuate the righteousness of God.

I go back to Joe as a great example of a disciple that was passionate about righteousness. Some say his many painful experiences when he lived a worldly life that indulged sin and unrighteousness caused him to adamantly oppose the unrighteous norm accepted in society today. But the truth is it was much more about his personal relationship with Christ. The one time I saw Joe let down his guard was when we had a professor from a major Christian university on a mission team in Guatemala. Keep in mind that we were working among a very poor people group that could not progress out of their poverty mainly due to their indulgence of alcohol.

The professor was attempting to get the area career missionary to take a more tolerant view of alcohol use. He was advocating that if the missionary, as the man of God and peace, would view the use of alcohol as an adult action rather than a societal wrong, the people as a whole would be better off because the teens would be less apt to want it. His argument was that it would be seen as something that old people do to forget their troubles and young people do not need because they are strong. Joe listened intently while this man pitched his propaganda. When he opened his mouth, it was with a passionate voice that he spoke, a voice that, if you had not known Joe, would have left you with a less than meek, humble view of Joe.

I will not go into the details of the argument, but in the end Joe looked the man in the eyes and said, "You are here to represent Jesus Christ and if your relationship with Him were mature you would see the wrong in your understanding and I will pray to that end." This argument may have sounded petty to many, but to Joe, this man had the gift of training young minds in a university that carried the name of Jesus. He had an obligation to view the use of alcohol in a society that worships alcohol as unrighteous in the eyes of God.

That was a point when I saw a meek man turn passionate about a societal wrong. With Joe, it was all the way or not at all. He was even more passionate when unrighteousness attacked the Gospel. He was completely intolerant of religions that directly alter the Gospel of Jesus and grace. I learned just how passionate for righteousness Joe was when his sister-in-law, who had married into a Catholic family, had a one-year-old child who was going to be christened, the first requirement of salvation according to the Catholic Church. Joe was the child's godfather and Joe loved this child and this family. However, for Joe to participate in this event would have made him a hypocrite and made his belief in the Gospel and the grace of Jesus Christ as the sole means of salvation more or less a farce.

Joe humbly stood his ground, even when his wife begged him, with many tears, to forget his views and do it for the sake of the family. She argued that someday he would have an opportunity to share the Gospel with this family and they would accept it because he had accepted their traditions. Joe would never intentionally hurt this family and it killed him inside to see his wife this upset, but he would not, could not let the unrighteousness of the Catholic doctrine make a farce of God's Word, God's Son, God's Gospel. I was a disciple-in-training stuck in the middle of this event learning what it really meant to hunger and thirst for righteousness. As a result, I can tell you this hunger for righteousness is not taught in a classroom by a disciple maker. It is learned through an intimate, personal relationship with Jesus Christ.

"Blessed are the merciful, for they shall receive mercy." (Matthew 5:7) When we teach "blessed are the merciful," we must be very clear as to what Jesus is and is not teaching here. There are some, even among Bible believers, that want to point to this verse and call it a contradiction to grace. Jesus is not teaching about how we receive the gift of salvation by grace, primarily because we do not have the power to obtain salvation nor do we have the power to give salvation. Jesus is teaching that if we show mercy to those who cannot help themselves, God will all the more forgive our sinful human nature here and now as well as reward or bless our actions on the day our works as believing children of God are reviewed.

I often have served on disaster-relief feeding and cleanup teams and, if we really want to understand what it means to extend Godly mercy, we have to be where people have nothing left except the clothes on their back. The helpless feeling of losing everything is powerful enough to cause a true Christian to extend a helping hand. But as disciples, it causes us to drop our all-important lives and go help those in need. A disciple of Jesus doesn't judge whether or not the person deserves help. He simply denies himself and helps. The reward is really irrelevant to one who acts out of true compassion and Jesus' Spirit living in them. So in truth, God is pleased and blessed when we are obedient to His own Spirit living in us that causes us to do what Jesus would do.

There is no greater reward for a child of God than for the Father to be pleased with us when we are obedient to His Spirit. However, don't think that just because God's Spirit lives in us, we have to be obedient. We don't. That's why we are called "children" and not "slaves." We can be sure that, no more than we would reward our children for ignoring our desires and failing to help someone in need, will God ignore our disobedience to His desire for His disciples to show mercy to the helpless and needy. After all, we are representatives of Christ and He showed the ultimate act of mercy when He stepped out of glory to save the helpless.

Blessed are the pure in heart, for they shall see God." (Matthew 5:8) I often have to examine my own heart and motives when I am called upon to show mercy or teach the truth concerning the God-like attitude of being pure in heart. This is another one of those characteristics that is easily overlooked and often taken for granted, mainly because it is easy to judge a person as meek by their demeanor and response to stressful situations and it is even easier to watch someone's actions when confronted with a person that is truly in need. But just like all the other beatitudes, Jesus teaches that maintaining a pure heart is a choice.

When I think of an experience in which I learned the meaning of "pure in heart" through another brother's action, I go back to my early twenties and a close friend of my father, Monty. The people that knew him closely knew that his faith was incredibly strong and that God had entrusted him with the gift of praying, anointing with oil, and healing. But ask him and you would never get an "I have" response. In fact, I don't believe he ever flat out requested that he be allowed to go pray for and anoint anyone. People that knew of his gift would call upon him to come to the bed of a sick person, but he never sought it out like the TV faith healers.

    I first learned of his pure heart when my father and the wife of one of his close friends called on Monty to come pray, anoint, and ask for healing of her husband who was awaiting a heart transplant. They had a very small window of time in which to do the transplant and the man was running a high fever, a sure sign of infection which would prevent the doctors from doing the surgery. The man had already lost one opportunity due to fever and this was more than likely his last chance.

    Monty came and anointed the man with oil and prayed an earnest prayer for the man's fever to subside and for any infection to die out. Within minutes, the man's fever broke, the nurses prepped him and he was off to surgery. Later, this family was so grateful they tried to reward Monty. He refused. They tried on several occasions to gift him and he would simply say, "I only did what scripture commands us to do. God does the healing." I don't believe Monty ever would have gone to the hospital if he had been offered a reward or gift in advance. Monty's motive was simply to be obedient to God's Spirit and to follow His guiding Word. A person who chooses to be pure at heart will see God, just as Monty saw God heal this dying man. But even the desire to see God cannot be a part of one's motives if they are truly pure.

"Blessed are the peacemakers, for they shall be called sons of God." (Matthew 5:9) Most of my adult life I have been surrounded by "peacemakers." I believe the peacemaker is that person who guides others to God's peace. Some of them are truly peaceful, calm people, but I have to say that my very close friend and brother in Christ, Mike, is the real peacemaker example in my life. Mike is not always the calmest guy, but he's always the guy I watch to know how to react in a Godly manner. If we truly want peace, act like Jesus.

At times in my life I could not see the peace of God. Whether I was being too passionate or just too stubborn, wanting my own way, I don't know. But every time I am frustrated at myself or a situation that has stolen me away from God's peace, I go talk with Mike. Sometimes if he even hears that I'm struggling, he is knocking on my door willing to get his nose bloody if need be to head me back to God's peace. The second biggest decision I ever made was to surrender to ministry. At that time in my life, my construction business was booming and I was serving as interim leader of the ministry after Joe's death, which meant I was training leaders while on mission six to ten times a year.

While on mission and serving God, I was fine, but when I came home to my business, it was complete turmoil.

I loved construction but dealing with customers was another thing altogether. It got to the point that I literally hated to listen to my voicemail after having been on mission for a week. Mike and I met and prayed together weekly. One day he said to me, "Glen, don't be confused by thinking that the success of your business is God trying to show you His will." He said, "You need to forget everything except this: Follow the Peace." It was at that point that I knew what God really wanted and I was able to walk away from my business and commit to serve God on a full-time basis and that was where I truly found God's peace.

It would be easy to say that Mike just stated the obvious, but you had to know me and know my desire to be successful. Mike helped me wrestle through this time in my life not by leaning back and saying, "Oh well, if Glen is meant to be director of this ministry, God will make it happen," and praying to that end. He challenged my reasoning, my understanding and, eventually, he challenged my faith in Jesus. To him, God's peace was the only answer to the happiness of my spiritual life and he was willing to do whatever it took to make me see that. In the end, it changed both our lives in a drastically peaceful way. Mike never intentionally pushed me but he did point me, even drove me, to the place where I chose to follow God's peace. He has not become a son of God because he guides and helps others make peace with God, but when others see God use him mightily in their lives, they know for sure he is a son of God.

"Blessed are those who are persecuted for righteousness' sake, for theirs is the kingdom of heaven." (Matthew 5:10) As disciple makers, we need to continually remind ourselves and those we are teaching, that for God, righteous choices are not an option. A truly righteous God can only make righteous decisions. The real problem for us in learning the importance of being right with God requires us to make choices that go against our human nature. In other words, making righteous choices is what we do because that's what Jesus did and, to please God, we must follow His son's example. In our world, there have been many well-known and famous people who have lost their lofty position in life by making a single righteous choice. I don't believe that Jesus is talking about them. I believe Jesus was talking to men who would soon be persecuted for choosing a right relationship with him. However, if we consistently choose righteousness over tolerance, we will soon learn that even Christians will persecute us when your righteous choice contradicts the status quo.

Jesus knew that, as His disciples, these men, as well as anyone who chooses righteousness, would be called on at some point to stand against society and even the religious community. It is easy to accept that the world at large doesn't like the right choice of a righteous person. As Christians, persecution will come and preparing for that is a required action if we are to stay strong in our faith. Jesus definitely wants our righteous choices to stand out in the eyes of the non-Christian and we will please God even if we don't enjoy the way we are treated by our neighbors. But when we are a part of a church, our tendencies are to go with the flow and let those in leadership be judged for unrighteous choices. That is an excuse and in very simple terms, it won't fly with God. Jesus, in this teaching, is preparing these men to be persecuted by those seen as righteous in the community. In fact, if you choose to obey Christ and be a maker of disciples, you will no doubt ruffle feathers among some in your church. I encourage you to stay the course and trust God's Word. In the end, the Word of God will judge us all.

"Blessed are you when others revile you and persecute you and utter all kinds of evil against you falsely on my account." (Matthew 5:11) My personal belief is that making disciples is the only choice for someone who desires a right relationship with God. And, as disciples, we will be confronted with standing up for Jesus and choosing Him over many things that society will say is the right way to be and act. When we choose to stand with Jesus, we will quickly understand what being persecuted for the sake of Jesus means. But don't back down. Stand by each other and train disciples to be strong in the face of those who are afraid of righteous people and even more afraid of followers of Jesus.

All of Jesus' disciples were martyred. They died not because they knew Jesus was the Son of God, not because they had been seen at His side when He conducted miracles, and not because they stood by Him in the Garden when Judas and the soldiers came to arrest Him. They died because they refused to stop proclaiming Him as Lord! Believe it or not, true Disciples of Christ are still dying today because they refuse to denounce their Lord and more and more each day, Christians that claim Jesus as Lord are facing heavy persecution and hardship. This is not limited to third world countries or to persecution at the hands of radical Islam. I have served on mission in Mexico for many years and followers of Christ that turn their backs on their Catholic heritage are treated like dogs by their families and the priests often target them and force them to leave their homes and move away.

One group of Christians within an indigenous people called the Huichol has suffered many years of verbal and physical persecution. At one point, they were held captive and sentenced to death by the leaders of their people. This is not happening because they are marching against the pagan practices and traditions of their people group. It is happening because they are sharing their belief in Jesus and people's lives are being changed. Trust me, this will never be seen on Fox News or in any other media, but it is nonetheless happening in places all around us. How about you? What if the local police arrest you and drag you to court for claiming Jesus as Lord and sharing the Gospel? Are you willing to die for the name of Jesus? Those who have done so made that choice long before the persecution came.

Chapter 5

The Visible Righteous Life

"....let your light shine before others, so that they may see your good works and give glory to your Father who is in heaven." ~Jesus
(Matthew 5:16)

    I often refer to the Sermon on the Mount as the constitution of righteousness. Not necessarily because it should be viewed like a set of laws, But because it should be viewed as the most important teaching on how to have a right relationship with Christ/God. Many times I talk with people who think righteousness is all about living a good moral life. In fact most Christians can identify at least one person who stands out as being more righteous than others.

    In my life, there are two such people and their personalities were polar opposites of each other. The first was a man named Raymond whom I went to church with in West Texas. He was a deacon in my church and probably the iconic picture of a good ole boy. Raymond was so calm most of the time you had to touch him just to make sure his pump was still ticking. But if you were to ask anyone who the best person they knew was, they would, without a doubt, say Raymond.

Raymond was always helping someone in a crisis or maybe they just needed a hand crossing the street. It didn't matter to him who it was. He dropped what he was doing and helped. Raymond was also never on the wrong side of an issue. He stood up against every wrong and was a gentle as a lamb in dealing with others' feelings. For a time, I was a leader in a boys' and young men's ministry called "Royal Ambassadors." I asked Raymond to come share his testimony with the group. He did and I was taken aback as I heard his story. He grew up in a very non-religious home with alcoholic parents and terrible siblings. He decided he was never going to become like his family so he became extremely moral. He became the good ole boy I described. He married a highly moral woman and someone just like he wanted to be. However, she was a Christian and soon he found himself involved in church life.

He became very active in church and learned that church was the place for people with high morals. He became a leader and, because he was so moral, he was asked to be a deacon. He went on for a few years like this until a visiting preacher came to preach and for the first time in his life, someone told him he could not get to heaven by being moral or living his whole life as a good ole boy. Raymond was confronted with the fact that, though he lived a righteous life in the eyes of all onlookers, he did not have the Light of men in his life. Raymond realized he was lost and decided to swallow his pride and give his heart to

Christ. He told the boys he still lived a moral life but when he made Jesus Lord, good ole Raymond died and perfect Jesus was born in his life. He said, "Now, I can honestly say my light shines bright."

The second person, John, was one of those men who truly impacted my life and the lives of many others because of his incredible relationship with Christ. Jesus flowed out of him in such a way that other disciples all but begged to spend time around this guy. He was not preachy nor did he throw scripture out constantly. He just knew Jesus and regardless of who was near, they heard about his great Jesus. He was a good person just like Raymond, but John always pointed people to Jesus. I am not sure, but he could have been the one who brought on the phrase, "what would Jesus do," not because he asked the question, but because he lived and demonstrated Jesus daily and he would quickly tell others that Jesus changed his life.

Anytime you sat down in a restaurant with him, John was going to include the waiters and even management in his prayers. I served on mission with him and often he would approach the obvious sinners and ask them if he could introduce them to the Savior of the world. He would approach a complete stranger and, just through a minute of observation, he would create a bond of trust. Without even asking the person, he would have them engaged in a conversation about God and Jesus. He was amazing and it would be easy to say he was gifted or an artist at communicating the Gospel, but the real truth is, he simply loved Jesus and shared the greatest love of his life. He truly understood how important the light of his life was to everyone else.

These two men though similar in their morally good lives had very different motives. I would have never in a million years guessed that Raymond had never given his life to Christ. Everything about him said he was a Christian except for one very important truth that most never even questioned. Raymond never shared Jesus, never talked about God's Word or his relationship with God. He couldn't share what he didn't have and he never had the light of the world in order to bring glory to God the Father.

On the other hand John lived just as moral but never excepted recognition for anything but his relationship with Jesus. He pointed others to Christ before he helped and he share the Gospel from a point of personal understanding like only someone in a relationship with Jesus can.

Jesus wants His disciples to understand the **vital role they will play in evangelizing the world.** In the world at that time, salt was more valuable than money. Most people had very little access to salt and, while the disciples may have not fully understood what Jesus was trying to convey entirely, they did understand the value of salt. As we teach this truth to disciples, we must above all else help them understand the foundation of it. These few men, much like disciples today, were being trusted with the key to eternal life, the Gospel. How they lived their lives would make a huge difference in every segment of society. (See Matthew 5:13-16.)

As we make disciples, we need to walk through how a disciple's life causes him or her to be salt and light in the world. I have had the privilege of discipling a young man named Blake. He worked as a construction site superintendent for a family-owned company. It was primarily run by a husband and his wife and though they were highly moral and good people, Blake realized that neither had a relationship with Christ. At first, Blake played it cool and didn't reveal that he was a disciple of Christ. You could say he hid his faith. But he soon realized how much this couple needed Christ. He began with very small comments and statements that revealed he was a Christian. Then, instead of asking for vacation time, he began to ask for time off to go on mission. He realized they were open to talking about their spiritual beliefs and he looked for opportunities to share the truth of the Gospel.

When his boss man was diagnosed with a terminal cancer, he knew he had to be bolder. We talked on many occasions about being spiritually prepared to share scripture and Blake began to memorize key scriptures. Soon he realized that he had been given the privilege of being the example of Jesus to this family. A few weeks before the man died, Blake was able to share the Gospel with him and it was clear his boss had put his faith in Christ. But his family was still very lost. In preparation for the funeral, the family leaned very heavily on Blake because they had no church home. Blake was again given the opportunity to be salt and light in this family. Blake never had to be loud or be forceful. He simply became the essential element to enrich the lives around him.

Christ placed this truth lesson about salt as a pivot point in His teachings on a righteous life. It's up to us to understand that we must keep the bold belief that compels us to be visible Christian witnesses and sprinkle the salt of righteousness on the lives around us. But that's not where Jesus leaves it for the disciple. He challenges the disciples to understand that if a disciple's life is to be more than a preservative of righteous living, it must be a floodlight in the darkest of nights. Jesus describes a righteous life as if it were a city covering a distant hill that can be seen for miles and miles. The closer you get to a righteous life, the more it brightens the lives around it, just like a single light in a dark room lights up the entire place.

The real kicker is the way Jesus places the choice to live a visible, righteous life directly in the disciple's hands, making it up to us to choose to be in a right relationship. He did this by announcing to His disciples in Matthew 5:14, "You are the light of the world." I believe at that very moment Jesus turned and pointed to the crowd of lost miracle chasers. Second, He places the choice in their hands as to whether or not they will be visible or hidden by telling them that real righteousness cannot be hidden. Some (mainly Judas) among the disciples would not choose the righteous life. What I love most is how Jesus closes with the real motivation for visible righteousness: "To God be the glory."

CHAPTER 6

Making Righteous Choices and Decisions

"Everyone then who hears these words of mine and does them will be like a wise man who built his house on the rock."
~*Jesus*
(Matt. 7:24)

After identifying the attitudes that lead to a right relationship with God, Jesus now shifts in His sermon to the actions and decisions that are made when one is in a right relationship with God. He sets the stage for the rest of His lesson (sermon) and clearly explains the role the Old Testament Law will play in our righteous lives. However, keep in mind that when Jesus explains in Matthew 5:17 that He is the fulfillment of the Law, it flies in the face of all that His disciples and the Jewish community at large believe, mainly because they have been taught that the coming Messiah will do away with all laws and establish new ones.

As I listened to other Christians struggle to answer why the Ten Commandments are still important to our lives here and now, it became very clear to me just how few believers understand the purpose of the Commandments, especially after Christ has said we no longer live under the Law but under God's grace. As we teach others about the Law, we must clearly explain how important the Commandments are to the followers of Christ.

    I shared with you the story of Richard in the first part of this book. What I didn't share was the story of Nathan, Richard's first disciple. Nathan was a man who was very confused about scripture and had little or no real understanding of God's grace. He could not even separate an Old Testament story from New Testament times. In Nathan's mind, the Ten Commandments were written for us to be able to govern society regardless of which era or the times. He saw them as being used by God to punish man and, in his thinking, man still needed to be punished, including himself. He had no idea they were given to point man to salvation. (See Psalm 19:7.) When he learned that the Law was given to reveal the need for a sinless sacrifice because man could not keep the entire Law, he then was able to understand why Jesus came to rescue man from certain death and separation from God.

    Nathan did not have an understanding of God's grace until he first understood that man could not keep God's Laws and that because of this, death or eternal separation from God was the penalty to all men. Once Nathan understood that it was impossible for any man to save himself, he then could understand why God sent His only Son to die as a sacrifice for all men's sin. The truth found in Matthew 5:17 that Jesus' sinless life fulfilled what the Law required and that His sacrificial death on the cross paid the price for all men's breaking of the Law literally opened Nathan's eyes. The fact that trying to be a good man and keep the Ten Commandments only revealed his own hopelessness shocked Nathan. For the first time in his life, he realized the importance of Jesus fulfilling the Law to his personal salvation. At that point, Nathan began to hear God draw him to salvation.

As disciple makers, we must help others realize that had Jesus not been the fulfillment of the Law, His life would have merely served to add to the impossibility of man meeting the requirements of the Law and condemned us even further. For disciples, the Law is as necessary to our right relationship with God as water is to sustaining human life. So how do we teach others to observe and build obedience to God through a natural progression rather than a forced legal burden? The truth is, in our own power it is impossible to make others anything more than friends of ours. Yet if we are disciplined to continually return to Jesus' first and the all-important truth in Matthew 5:3 and realize we are completely dependent on Him and His Holy Spirit's work in us, we can and will lead others out of a life bound to sin and futile attempts to keep all of God's Law. There is one thing we must certainly keep in mind: Jesus was never arrogant or proud of the fact that He kept all of the Law and even when He does announce that He has fulfilled the Law, He does so privately with His disciples.

Over the years I have discovered that people have a great bit of difficulty accepting that Jesus is literally amending the big Ten that God gave Moses on Mount Sinai. However, to true disciples of the Master, He is seen as the very one with the authority to amend any law, and, as his disciples, we will see these amendments as having the same power as the original Ten Commandments. Many of the men I have helped become disciples have grown up with no understanding of these amendments. Nor do they have an understanding of what role the Ten Commandments, set forth in the Old Testament, play in our lives today. Even many who have heard the Sermon on the Mount preached throughout their lives do not give weight to the amendments made by Jesus because in truth they have never truly understood that grace does not void the commands of God.

It is true that it is much easier to believe you're good because you have not committed murder than it is to look in the mirror of life and say, "I have never been angry with anyone." (See Matthew 5:21-22.) In fact, some advocate that it is not in any way possible to fulfill these amendments, so it makes no sense that Jesus would add unrealistic requirements to an already difficult Law. But in truth, Jesus, in every amendment, is clarifying what perfection is. If the Law was intended to help us be perfect in the eyes of a perfect God and Creator, then we must realize that, through the Law, we will know perfection.

In the same sense, if God uses the Ten Commandments to teach us that we cannot fulfill the Law, then Jesus' amendments will make the Law all the more impossible for us to fulfill. This is why it is so critical that, as disciples, we understand this is the constitution of righteousness and that in our human nature it is impossible to be perfect. (See Romans 3:10.) These amendments teach us that this is the constitution of Jesus, the one and only perfect Son. Our hope is laid out here in this lesson. One day we will all be transformed into the image of Jesus, we will realize Matthew 5:48 and the perfection of God will be ours.

When, Jesus breaks from amending the Law in Matthew 5:21-6:4, he starts to shed light on our human nature and systematically goes through our emotional states of mind and common reactions to sin and the way we view ourselves. Jesus carries this thought into our actions and how we demonstrate our Christianity in front of the world around us. He even points out our motives in regard to prayer and fasting. When I first began to disciple others, prayer and, in particular the Lord's Prayer in Matthew 6:5-15, was the first place God began to teach me and deal with me to change the way I approached my own prayer life as well as how I taught others to view prayer.

One encounter I will never forget was with a person who had come on mission several times and, from all the visible accounts; she was rather caring and spiritually mature. One night I noticed the team leader avoiding her during a round-circle prayer in which everyone in the circle prayed out loud. She was standing next to him yet he skipped her and started the prayer with the person on her other side. He concluded the prayer time himself. Later I approached the team leader and learned this person refused to openly pray out loud. We did not discuss the reason, but I did ask if I could talk with her about it. He was in agreement that as the missionary I would be able to encourage her.

As the mission went on, I had time to talk with her and I shared that I was a student of prayer and I intended to be a student as long as I lived. At one point, she finally asked me a question that enabled me to share what Jesus teaches about prayer. In her case, as a small child she was taught that we should never pray in public and that the only proper way to truly communicate with God was alone in our "closet." I took her to the model prayer and we went through it step by step. She agreed that Jesus never says this is the only way to pray and on several occasions He instructs His disciples to openly pray as well. She acknowledged the numerous prayers of Jesus that took place in full view of those around Him. I asked her if she only talked with her husband when they were alone at home or whether they talked openly in public places.

The long and short of this event was that she learned that prayer (talking to God) is no different than talking to someone we love. We do learn more about them when we are in a private place and in a more intimate conversation. Yet if we never talk to them in any other place, we never learn who they truly are in public. I shared with her a time that I prayed before a meal, something she flatly refused to do, and a man at the other end of the table began to cry. He was under great conviction and God used this prayer of thanksgiving to show this man His love. I honestly do not remember the words of the prayer. Had I never prayed thanking God for his daily provisions, I would have never had the privilege of God speaking to this man's heart through my prayer.

That night at the dinner table in a crowded restaurant, she prayed for the evening meal. It was her first public prayer and she shared with me that she felt God's love as she prayed and that many of her team members were praying with her. She now understands the power of corporate prayer. Prayer is the single most important aspect of a disciple's life and we must be willing to help others learn who Jesus is as well as how He uses our prayers to teach us about Himself as well as grow our personal relationship with Him.

I must add this to my thought on prayer. Every disciple I have ever assisted on this disciple's road has had some issue with unforgiveness. If we do not understand every aspect of Jesus' model prayer, that is okay, but we must not miss the importance Jesus places on forgiveness in His Prayer. It is the key to effective communication with God. He makes it very clear we must forgive to be in a right relationship with Him.

As Jesus continues His lesson, He virtually walks us through the right choices to make in our many life decisions. For instance, we all want to be wealthy or at least experience wealth in our own individual ways. We will all have people and things of great importance (treasures) in our lives and how we view those will stand out in the minds of our friends and family. (See Matthew 6:19-24.) As a young man, I was just like all my non-believing friends. I wanted to be successful and have plenty of toys. It was a competition between friends that we never discussed. We just strived to get as much as we could and kept one eye on our friends to make sure we were slightly ahead. I never once stopped to ask, "Is God pleased with all of this?"

But in my late twenties, God used a tragic event to wake me up to the reality that He wanted to be the most important person/thing in my life. I had learned so little about following God and a relationship with Him that I became hungry to learn and grow up spiritually. After this tragic event occurred, I attended every conference, every service and every teaching event that came into our area or that was associated with our church. I began to grow and see God leading me into a greater understanding.

One event that really stood out in my mind happened in one of those church-wide teaching events. At one point in the lesson, the subject of treasures was being discussed. An older and very well-known and respected man in our church, B.R. James, was sitting in the pew in front of me. He was a humble and likeable senior man. I did not know his story, but I did know he was a fairly wealthy man.

When the focus shifted from earthly treasures to heavenly treasures, Mr. James stood and asked if he could share his testimony with the group. He had been a very successful commercial building contractor and most of his youthful years were spent building and acquiring wealth. He listed much of what he had accumulated. He told of how these things dominated his life even over the continued success of his company. He worried and thought about how to protect his material possessions to the point that he became constantly paranoid that he was going to lose them. He described how his possessions took first place in his life until one day he suffered a massive heart attack and barely survived to be at that event.

He had grown up in church and remained faithful to every aspect of the Christian life except in one area. He only very seldom gave an offering to the church. He just didn't see the value in giving to Kingdom work. When he had the heart attack, he died several times on the operating table. He told how God spoke to him during those moments. He saw no light. He saw nothing. In fact, he said God pointed him to the fact that he was about to enter eternity with nothing. He had more toys than anyone he knew but not one treasure in heaven. He said the one thing about this experience that changed his heart was that even though he had no treasure and nothing that said "heaven is my home," Jesus loved him anyway.

When he recovered from heart surgery, Mr. James sold most of his toys, two vacation homes and all but two of his cars. He began to give to the Kingdom work. He lost all his paranoia, all his fear of losing his earthly wealth and gained a love for God and the things of God to the point that on that day he was able to tell everyone, "I love Jesus first and most of all." Jesus does not demand we give Him money and part of our wealth. He simply demonstrates through His life that we are His treasure and He paid the ultimate price to make us His eternal treasure. I do not want to stand before my Lord who loves me unconditionally and have absolutely no treasure or way to express my love for Him.

In Matthew Chapter 7, Jesus no doubt strategically addresses how we judge others right behind how we view wealth and motives. This is one place we have to get it right to be right with God. He will go on to teach us what we should judge, but He clearly teaches that judging the motives of others is wrong and, as His followers, we are not to judge others in this way. We must be mindful that if we judge men's motives it will hinder the sharing of the Gospel. Yes, some will not accept our testimonies or hear the Gospel, but if we judge others as disinterested or rebellious before we share the Gospel, we will more than likely not share with someone who would have received it.

We need to understand that Jesus is the source of all righteous choices and, although He points out those choices, the truth is, we must recognize how much we need Him in order to ever make them. He emphasizes that by teaching us that, as we strive to live the Godly life of a disciple, we must learn and practice asking, seeking, and knocking on His door for the power to make righteous choices. (See Matthew 7:7-11.) We must never sell the importance of this sermon short. If disciples do not understand this is who Jesus is, these are the choices He makes, and this is the way of His followers, we will always discount its importance and miss out on having a whole relationship with Jesus. He points out how men have the desire to care for and give to their children, then He places Himself in the higher position of the Almighty God who will certainly not withhold a single blessing from His children.

From childhood we are told be kind to others, but Jesus takes that one step further when He gives what we have come to know as the Golden Rule, when He says, "So whatever you wish that others would do to you, do also to them for this is the Law and the Prophets." (Matthew 7:12) He adds an emphasis that ties this to the very basis of all of God's Law.

As we seek to share the Gospel and make disciples, we will learn, sometimes the hard way, that following Jesus will be a very difficult way. Many of our fellow Christians will claim to be on the narrow road and understand this hard way of living, but Jesus tells us that very few will truly travel this narrow, hard and lonely life. As a disciple maker, I will tell you that even most of your Christian friends and family will not accept the life of a disciple or your message as a disciple maker. You will find this is the hardest part of this narrow road.

What often is not discussed about the Golden Rule is that Jesus does not say, "Do unto others as you would have them do to you, *and they will.*" The bare, hard truth is that you will be viewed as strange when you go out of your way to help others. And when you stand firm in your decision to do as Jesus dictates that we do in this passage, you more often than not will stand all alone in a crowd of Christians. These men may not have fully understood at that time what Jesus was telling them, but they soon learned, just as we will learn. Following the ways of Jesus is the most difficult choice we will ever make.

Near the conclusion of His lesson Jesus warns His disciples about how many will abuse and use His name for self-gain and to produce self-gratifying fruit. (See Matthew 7:15-20.) Be careful about thinking this is all about TV evangelists and preaching profiteers. Many times it will simply be a person within the family circle, a person within your own church who doesn't necessarily draw a crowd of cheerers. They simply use their God-given gifts to manipulate others to get what they want out of life. Jesus gives us one sure-fire way to know false Christians. He tells us to examine their fruit. If they are leaving hurt and broken people in their wake, don't be fooled into believing they are concerned about your spiritual wellbeing.

Jesus makes one of the strongest emphasis in all of scripture when He closes His lesson with two prophesies. The first is a revelation of how many Christians are satisfied with who they have become in the church and their busy actions in the name of Jesus but in their own power, and that it will be revealed that Jesus was not in them and therefore He never knew them. On that day, He will be forced to send them to a place of separation from Him, because, in truth, they followed their own set of laws, not those in the constitution of righteousness. (See Matthew 7:21-23.)

The second prophesy concerns how we view this constitution. If we refuse to follow these fundamental instructions of Jesus concerning our spiritual lives, we will experience the greatest crushing blow of all when our lives are tested by the storm. However, if we heed Jesus' teachings, build our faith in Him, remain completely dependent on Him, and travel the narrow road with Him, we will recognize Satan's sandpit, rejoice and find a solid foundation and eternal life in Christ. (See Matthew 7:24-27)

PART 3

A Disciple's View of
Evangelism

*"Go into all the world and proclaim the gospel
to the whole creation"*
~Jesus
(Mark 16:15)

Chapter 7

Living an Evangelistic Lifestyle

"I have been crucified with Christ. It is no longer I who live, but Christ who lives in me. The life I now live in the flesh, I live by faith in the Son of God, who loved me and gave himself for me."
~Paul
(Galatians 2:20)

I have a good friend with whom I have had a close relationship for the last 25 years. He loves the Lord and is a student of scripture and someone with whom I often share my love of God and relationship with Jesus. However, he has a strong passion for guns as well as a vast knowledge of them. Now don't misunderstand me. *He doesn't worship guns in any way*, but whenever he and I are going to spend time together, I have no doubt that at some point we will be in a deep discussion about guns. I also know that if we encounter another friend or acquaintance of his, at least 90 percent of the time, guns will be the topic of the conversation. People who know him know he is an authority on all types of firearms and if they ask him a question, they will almost certainly get the correct answer.

Over the years, I have watched his life take many turns and change in several ways, but none more exciting to me than that of his personal relationship with Christ. When we first met, our children were very young. In fact, my twin daughters were not yet born. Early in our friendship, I spent a considerable amount of time working with him and I will say we talked Bible a lot, but we seldom if ever talked about our relationships with Christ. I did learn something, however, that set me on a path toward the truth of the Gospel. We were having one of those days where we were testing each other's views and beliefs. I shared my view of the Gospel as something every born-again believer has a responsibility to share. He agreed, but his view of disciple making was far different than mine. In his view, sharing our faith was the end of our responsibility as Christians. I held the view that making disciples was a process and we have a responsibility to go with others through that process.

At the time, my greatest need was to know scripture and write it on the walls of my heart. God made my need perfectly clear. I learned my good friend believed our responsibilities were limited to sharing our faith and leaving the rest to God. The truth is, way back then, I couldn't really give him a clear reason to believe differently or take a look at our responsibilities as disciple makers rather than as evangelists. His comments stirred something up in my heart and I began to seek a greater understanding of why I was so compelled to share my faith and see others become disciples. In that pursuit, I learned just how much Jesus loves me and how He wanted to have a personal relationship that was very unique to me as an individual. However, it would be 20 years before I would be seen as a disciple maker to my friend. Today, he has become one of my closest spiritual brothers and we often have deep spiritual conversations and share our love for God's Word.

I use our early relationship as an example because, unfortunately, it is typical within the American church community. I say that because the church house is the growing place of the American Christian and the very key reason churches have many more people on the church rolls than actually attend church on a consistent basis. That is what drew me to begin to question and study my friends. I came to realize almost every Christian I knew was passionate about something other than Jesus Christ.

Every Sunday morning before Bible study there was a fellowship time. If we came early or on time, we had several minutes to interact with friends and fellow believers. I often just walked around the room greeting folks and listening to their conversations. Let me tell you, if you want info on everything from football and hunting to where to eat or the best dress shop in town, go to Sunday morning Bible study and take a recorder. You will get way too much information to ever write it all down.

At some point, I was compelled to put on my spiritual ears and listen for spiritual matters just as if I were Jesus Himself. This was a life-changing moment for me. The room, full of people talking, became utterly silent and even though it appeared that every mouth in the room was moving, my ears were frighteningly deaf. Not until the prayer before the actual study began did I hear a single word spoken of spiritual matters, and even more frightening, I never heard the name of Jesus come out of anyone's mouth! Sad, but true, and common in every church in America. My life has never been the same and God used this period to teach me how to help others develop an evangelistic lifestyle, a lifestyle that is passionate about the person of Jesus and sharing our relationship with the King of Kings and Lord Almighty.

I firmly believe that our faith can and should be at the heart of every conversation we have. I am not saying we should never talk about sports, fashions, or politics. But when we start our conversations with a subject that is disconnected from our faith, we seldom if ever get the conversation to a place where we can share our faith experiences, especially when we know the person we are talking to may have never heard the Gospel before. It is even more critical to our personal relationship with God that we be comfortable with faith-related conversations within the walls of His house, our church settings.

I believe every true disciple of Christ is compelled by God's Holy Spirit to share the Gospel with a lost world and their personal relationship with Christ with other Christian believers. In fact, Jesus Himself said the very same thing in Acts 1:8. Just before He ascended into the heavens, He gave a promise and a command to go with the promise. "But you will receive power when the Holy Spirit has come upon you (the promise), and you will be my witnesses in Jerusalem and in all Judea, and Samaria, and to the ends of the earth (the command)." But hear me closely: If we as disciple makers do not share our personal experiences with Christ and Gospel-sharing moments with our fellow believers at church, we will never be confident or comfortable with sharing the Gospel to those who have never heard it anywhere outside the safe walls of the church house.

The very first step before a person will and can share the Gospel of Jesus is to love Him. You show me a Christian that truly loves the Lord and I will show you a bold witness of God Almighty. I am reminded of my mother every time I talk about loving God. My mother loved the Lord so deeply that she sought Him as the greatest treasure of her life. Even when she suffered a stroke and could no longer speak, she shared her love for him every chance she had. She took Gideon New Testaments and handed them to people folded open to the last page, which is a presentation of the Gospel. She would hold her finger on the page as the person took her gift and motion with her smile for them to read it. Most did and one day in heaven we will see the many lives that she impacted for the name of Jesus. My mother never went on a mission trip, she never preached in a pulpit, and she never forced her beliefs on a single person. Even so, she shared the Gospel more times every year than 90 percent of all preachers, deacons or missionaries. And this was not because she felt obligated or appointed, and certainly not because she wanted the recognition of the religious community. She simply shared the greatest love of her life because she wanted others to know Him and love Him also.

So, how do we lead others to love the Lord? Just like we learned to love our mother, our spouse, or any other person that we truly have a loving relationship with. We bring them into our relationship and permit them to spend time with our loving Lord. Today's method of handing a person a book or Bible and telling them to read at least two chapters a day is not at all an example demonstrated in scripture. I don't care what seminary you attended, nowhere in all the Bible will you find a Godly man or disciple that became one without spending time getting to know the person of Jesus. Again, don't twist what I'm saying. It is impossible to know God and spend time with Jesus without much time spent in scripture! However, as disciple makers we must follow the example of Christ as He made His disciples. He invited every one of them to follow Him. He didn't mean on Facebook or Twitter. He meant for them to spend all day, every day with Him.

Maybe we can't expect a person to move in and live with us, but we can spend adequate time each week with them for them to see and know our personal relationship with Jesus. Through time spent with them, we can help them see God drawing them and interacting with them on a personal basis. If we truly love the Lord with all our heart, it will be contagious and anyone who spends time with us will be infected with our love for God. The disciples were infected by Jesus' love for His Father and when they saw

Him pray, it was not just a chit chat with a mystical being. It was an event! It was a powerful event that changed every situation and impacted every life involved in the event. If Jesus is in us, our personal relationship with Him and genuine love for God will infect others who desire to know God in a greater way.

The second practice we must develop is to talk in church with other believers about our experiences of sharing the Gospel and our faith. If we truly love God more than sports, eating and shopping, then our conversations in God's house should reflect that. If we want to help others become evangelical, we need to teach them that it is okay to discuss faith matters. It is okay to openly share your passion for Christ. When we become comfortable sharing our faith experiences with other believers in church, it will translate into a greater boldness to live evangelically every moment of our lives.

The greatest obstacle to living an evangelical lifestyle is to make sharing our faith a special event, especially when that event is designed and planned around only sharing the Gospel and our testimony. For many years, I have been leading short-term mission teams into foreign countries to do evangelism. My experience has taught me that most of those who come on mission are prepared to share the Gospel and their personal testimony through a memorized or often a written method. I'm not putting down those people. If that's the only way a person knows how to share the Gospel, that's how they should share it. However, the fact is that most of the missionaries that come with these methods do so because they are not comfortable sharing what they believe about Jesus.

As disciple makers, it's our privilege to lead folks into a greater personal relationship with the person of Jesus Christ. If you ask any of those folks to tell you about their family, I promise you they won't pull a scripted message out and recite it. Our goal is to help others who desire to be disciples of Christ have a powerful, on-going relationship with Christ so that they are as comfortable sharing who He is to them as they are about sharing their family. In other words, we need to lead fellow Christians into a relationship with Jesus in which He becomes one of their loved ones, in fact, their most beloved one.

I have noticed that very few of those who share the Gospel through a memorized or scripted method ever share their faith in the communities in which they live every day. Something about going a long way away from our comfort zones gives us a sense of confidence that permits us to pull out a written script or recite a canned speech containing the Gospel that we absolutely would never do in the context of our comfortable communities we live in. Maybe it's because we know we are going home and these folks will likely never see us again or it might be the language barrier and thinking they don't really understand us anyway. But one thing is for sure, a very small percentage of those with canned methods ever share their faith when they return home. When a disciple maker sees this, he has an obligation to help that brother or sister get to know Christ as one of their loved ones. In doing so, we enable them to begin a lifestyle of evangelism.

What I am saying is that when we have a relationship with the person of Jesus that resembles the ones we have with the love of our life and our loved ones, we will be much more verbal about that relationship. We will also transfer the habits of how we naturally share our relationship with our loved ones into how we share our relationship with God. Just like we use phrases such as my wife, my husband, my son, or my daughter in announcing our relationships with our loved ones, we will use phrases like my God, my Lord, my Savior or even my Jesus.

A great little self-examination exercise is to count the number of times in a day that you refer to one of your close relationships in a passing conversation. In other words, don't go out of your way to say or not say certain phrases about those with whom you have a relationship. Simply be yourself and review your conversation later in your mind. It might just surprise you how easy transferring that habit into sharing your relationship with Jesus really is. Maybe a better description would be how easy including Jesus in that habit will be. It might also help you see just how little we share anything about our relationships period.

Recently, I was eating lunch with a missionary whom I have known for many years. I have been a mentor to him and we have talked extensively about our relationship with Jesus and how those relationships have infected our everyday conversations. While we were eating lunch and visiting, I noticed him including phrases that announced his relationship with Jesus much more boldly and as if he wanted people to ask him what he meant. At one point, a young man he knew walked up to our table and greeted us. Luis asked him how he was doing and if he knew how much Jesus loved him. The man was not surprised by this. He answered with a "Yes sir, I really do." He asked Luis how he was and Luis answered him with "absolutely great" and added, "It is a great day to spend with Jesus." The young man said, "Okay, what do you want to tell me?"

Luis told him to sit down and he began to share an experience he had with Jesus the day before:

> "I was writing a report for seminary class and I became burdened that God had not used me in anyone's life recently so I stopped and prayed for a while. When I started back on the paper I just couldn't stop repeating the prayer in my mind, 'God please use me in someone's life today.' Near midday, I was still working on the paper and praying when I heard a knock at my gate outside. When I went to investigate, there was a young man waiting there. He told me he was in need and was wondering if I could help him. I asked him what his need was. The young man became emotional and said his child had died the day before and his priest said it would cost him $35 for a

penance in order for the Catholic Church to obtain the child's release from purgatory. I told the man, 'I will give you the money but you need to know I don't believe in this practice and I would like to tell you what God's Word says about this and about all children.' The man was actually eager to hear, so I brought out my Bible and began to show him. I also shared the Gospel with him and he excitedly asked Jesus into his heart and surrendered his life to Jesus. When the man walked away with the $35 and a New Testament, I fell to my knees and praised God because He heard my cry to be with Him today and had chosen to let me be a part of His redeeming work in this young man's life."

I tell this story because when we have a relationship with Jesus that is visible and in real time, we can't wait for others to hear about our experiences with Him. Because the young man's response to Luis' experience was, "I wish I had those types of experiences to share," Luis invited this young man to meet with him every week and permit him to help him become a true disciple of Jesus. Just a few years ago, Luis was just like this man and God gave me the privilege of guiding him and making him a true disciple maker. Today, Luis is a confident witness of God everywhere he goes, not because I spent time with him as much as because God chose to draw Luis to Himself through me and I was obedient to share the disciple's relationship I had with Jesus. The glory for the results is all God's and He alone is Luis' Lord. However, I am extremely blessed to see that Luis has an incredible, visible relationship with Jesus that has made him a true disciple maker.

All of us will encounter fear and intimidation in regard to sharing the Gospel. For this reason, we must combine our love for Christ with knowledge of the Gospel and become very comfortable discussing and explaining our faith and personal relationship with God. In *The Carpenter's Guide, Part 3: A Disciple's View of Evangelism,* a lot of time will be spent on learning how to share and become comfortable sharing the Gospel as well as your personal story and relationship with Christ. Many believers in your own church have never discussed the Gospel in a personal manner inside or outside of the church. By using our church as an incubator or training place, we can grow our confidence and comfort level in a more-or-less safe place. At the same time, we will discover just how many in our church need and want the same confidence and comfort we are building.

What is most interesting is that as we become more and more confident and comfortable sharing the Gospel and your story with other believers, that confidence will naturally take over in situations where we know we are talking to a nonbeliever. When we become comfortable and confident in our own church, the practice of sharing will become our naturally evangelistic lifestyle with very little effort. Just think about it this way: Jesus spent a year and a half with His disciples, preparing them and allowing their love for Him to grow and their faith in Him to become confident before He ever let one of them go out and proclaim the Gospel. This alone should be an adequate example for us to grow within the church in order to be confident outside of the church.

With that said, we must understand that when we are at church, we need to be intentional about sharing our faith experiences. By doing so, we will be preparing to live an evangelical lifestyle outside the church. In turn, our comfort and confidence will become a huge asset for God to draw unbelievers to Himself through us. In short, we should spend much time discussing and practicing how we share the Gospel for the sole purpose of going out and sharing the Gospel with non-believers and returning to share that experience with other believers. This becomes the primary function of the church for a disciple. It was the function of the early church and should be the primary function of all local churches today. The local church should be preparing itself to be on the mission of sharing the Gospel daily rather than preparing a handful of its members for an event or to go on a short-term mission once a year.

The mission of the church becomes Acts 1:8-like because all of the church is prepared to share the Gospel and bear witness of their relationships with Christ confidently and daily. This will result in a natural fulfillment of Jesus' command in Acts 1:8: "...you will be my witnesses in

Jerusalem and in all Judea and Samaria, and to the end of the earth." The church will be mobilized in the community, and wherever the disciples go, whether to school, work, shopping, on vacation, or to a specified mission place or people, they will be God's witness from home to the ends of the earth. When evangelical disciples are themselves, then wherever they are, God is glorified, He draws the lost to Himself through us, and the church lives an Acts 1:8 lifestyle.

For many years, I have incorporated three methods of sharing the Gospel into my personal story. I believe more people understand the simple but very visible method of *The Bridge* presentation because it touches on the basic belief that people who are good, have good family, or are even religious families and help others will be rewarded with eternal salvation. Believe it or not, even people (not terribly bad people) who have never gone out of their way to help even their own loved ones tend to believe that God will not send them to hell for doing nothing. *The Bridge* allows us to expose people's beliefs that being good, religious or church members will not get them to heaven and allows us to get to the truth very quickly.

However, *The Bridge* is not a great conversation starter. Often, we need to slow down and ask a few qualifying questions. This is where *Share Jesus Without Fear* becomes an amazing tool to quickly determine if a person is ready to receive the Gospel or whether we should simply pray for them and move on. In addition, this method uses some fundamental sociology to help the person discover the truth of the Gospel on their own. When we share our Bible with someone and ask them to read a verse of scripture with us, we put them at ease and at the same time give them the impression that they are in control and can stop at any point. In other words, *Share Jesus Without Fear* works to calm the person down and helps them not feel threatened by our questions. This is also a very easy way to lead into a clearer explanation using a more visible method to solidify what they have already discovered on their own.

When we encounter situations in which we have very little time, the quick presentation of the *ABC Method* is quite good. It may fall short of a complete explanation, but it is a great way to plant a solid seed and often leads to the person stopping and giving you adequate time to fully share the Gospel. We must keep in mind that the goal of every opportunity to share the Gospel is to make a disciple. Matthew 28:18-20 is a clear command to make disciples. Sharing the Gospel is the beginning step of making disciples. However, without a plan to make a disciple of every person that receives salvation, we fall far short of fulfilling Jesus' command.

As disciple makers, we teach others to become confident and comfortable in sharing the Gospel, but in almost every Gospel presentation method, the key element of our personal story is not there. One might assume that we will share our story at every chance. This is one of the reasons so few people ever share the Gospel. In church, we might attend an evangelism class and we will learn a method or way to share the Gospel. Often we will learn dozens of verses to use, if not more, and they are all good. But we are seldom, if ever, taught to share our story and our personal relationship with Christ. We should never assume that our story and personal relationship with Jesus is not relevant to the Gospel or that those we are teaching will get lost in their own story and never get to the Gospel. The key to helping others become comfortable, confident and effective in sharing their faith story and an evangelical lifestyle is to give (teach) them as many tools as they need but not so many they become confused.

In order to make disciples, we must be willing to invest in others' lives and do more than lead them in a sinner's prayer, then drop them at the doorstep of the church. It will take an evangelical lifestyle that loves our Lord more than we love ourselves and understands that the goal is not to merely lead a person to faith but to **draw others to faith in Christ and guide them into a personal relationship with Jesus. This is what true disciple making is.** When we understand that an evangelical lifestyle is to be a disciple maker, we will stop counting numbers and start spreading the love of God on thick.

PART 4

Go Make
Disciples

"If anyone would come after me, let him deny himself and take up his cross daily and follow me."
~Jesus
(Luke 9:23)

Chapter 8

Getting Started Making Disciples

"All authority in heaven and on earth has been given to me. Go therefore and make disciples of all nations...."
~Jesus
(Matthew 28:18-19)

As we endeavor to follow Jesus' example of making disciples, it is critical that we understand that He did nothing randomly or based on happenstance. Jesus came with a strategic plan to grow up an army of disciples that would take the Gospel (the power of God – see Romans 1:16) and make it known to all men. The details of this strategy are made known to us in His words and actions throughout the New Testament. His plan does not begin with Him announcing who He is or a demonstration of His power through miracles. He comes as a simple carpenter and He is first made known by the voice of John the Baptizer. He does not command men to follow Him. Instead, He approaches a very small group of men to come follow Him. In other words, He *invites* them to be a part of His everyday life.

Through time spent with Him, a bond of trust was built. There is no doubt Jesus could have chosen these men through a powerful direction of His divine Spirit to do as He commanded as nothing more than puppets. After all, He was God. But if He had used His Godly powers in that manner, how would you and I take that example today and repeat it? We could not. He came as a man that we might be able to follow His human example. He invited men that He *knew* were teachable and willing to follow Him and learn the strategy. They believed He was the Messiah, yet He proved who He was to them by the miraculous catch of fish. When they saw His power for the first time, they then abandoned their daily routines and followed Him.

Jesus made only one promise at that moment. He promised He would make them fishers of men. There is no doubt in my mind that these men did not fully understand His promise. They were very common-sense men that simply put two-and-two together and recognized that Jesus was the Messiah they had been waiting for. In other words, they wanted a relationship with Him. This alone is the most overlooked truth in scripture. Think about it. The entire Jewish community was looking for a Messiah that would lead them by the power of God to a victorious battle over their oppressors. But Jesus didn't come as a commander of armies. He did not resemble a military general nor did He even carry so much as a pocket knife in which to attack the enemy. He was clearly not what these men had been led to believe the Messiah would be. Yet, for some mysterious reason, they abandoned their lives and followed Him.

For some number of years, I had disciple making completely backwards and I made many illegitimate attempts to make men that I knew into the disciples I believed they needed to be. I selected them by their desire to be religiously upright, faithful in church attendance and extremely moral men. What I failed to see was that though they were faithful leaders in their church, few of them felt the need for a personal relationship with Christ. They had invested heavily in their positions in the local church and, to them, it would have been a huge step backwards to start down a new path that might jeopardize their positions and bring radical changes to their status quo, especially when that might mean lowering themselves to follow or be a part of a man's life that, like Jesus, had no religious title or credentials.

Please don't misunderstand me. God will most often use our local church relationships to draw those willing and able to be His disciples into our lives. I am simply saying that it is not always the most visible person in the church that God is drawing and we must remain humble and let God do the drawing rather than choose the one we see as spiritually hungry.

For some time, I studied to find out who in my local church would make a disciple and who would desire to spend time with me in the pursuit of becoming a disciple. One man emerged as a likely candidate. This man was a humble, quiet servant who was often called upon to be a part of leadership functions in the church. He was one of those guys that seldom dominated a conversation but everyone was slightly curious as to what he thought. I first began to study his life because of a pattern that developed between us within our Bible study hour on Sunday mornings. The teacher would almost always drag his lesson into a political or materialistic direction. Most of the time, this would bring on some spirited discussion but seldom leave room for spiritual application.

Being the director of a parachurch ministry, I was not in Bible study on a weekly basis, but every time I was in town, I was there. One week after I had missed two or three lessons, this man came up to me before the class and asked me how the ministry was going. At first, I thought he was genuinely interested in learning how God uses this ministry. I shared a brief testimony and he said he would love to hear more about it sometime. I walked to my seat thinking God was showing me that this man was either already a disciple or wanted to be a disciple. This was the beginning of a period in which he would come to me weekly and ask why our ministry does certain things. One Sunday I invited him to have lunch so I could share with him in detail what God had called us to do.

When he said to me, "I don't need to know all that much. I just wondered why your ministry takes precedence over this church's ministry," it was the first time I realized his motive. His response fooled me because I truly believed he was interested in me and God's work. In fact, I met with him a couple of times. On one of those occasions I asked him straight out if he was a disciple or if that was something he was not sure of and wanted to find out. As it turned out, this very humble and kind man was all he believed I and every other church member should be. He believed spiritual maturity was only evident in consistent, faithful church attendance. He told me disciples were only relevant today in that they pointed lost men to the church where they could repent and be baptized for the forgiveness of their sins. He made it sound so matter of fact that I had no reason to question him any further. I wish this was the only encounter of this nature I could relate here, but the truth is, his attitude is much more prevalent than any other. Even so, his attitude is not a good reason to abandon the local church and stop seeking to make disciples through our church relationships.

We, as churches on a local community level, need to learn how the church makes disciples together and then we need to be about our Father's business. John Chapter 14 is a key passage of scripture regarding how a relationship with God works. We should pay close attention in particular to Jesus' description of how He and God the Father function as one. When we understand how the relationship between Jesus and God the Father works, we gain greater understanding into how our relationships will function in unison with God the Father and Jesus Christ as one. The very clear truth that jumps out at our selfish ears is that Jesus and God in us will function best when we together, as the disciple-making church, function as one.

The truth is, Jesus was working His strategy step-by-step to make known the Gospel message and His plan of redemption for all who place their faith in Him. He knew that for us to ever make the redeeming Gospel message known throughout the world, we would need help. Many times I have stood behind someone sharing the Gospel and prayed John 14:12-14: "Truly, truly, I say unto you, whoever believes in me will also do the works that I do; and greater works than these will he do, because I am going to the Father. Whatever you ask in my name, this I will do, that the Father may be glorified in the Son." With all the faith I could muster, I would pray the promise back to Jesus knowing that the eternal destination of the listener did not hinge on the adequate words of the one sharing the Gospel but on the saving power of Christ alone. To me, this is the key passage for every evangelistic missionary to keep on the tip of his or her tongue, knowing that unless Jesus draws and saves the person we share the Gospel with; all our convincing words and tiresome efforts are in vain.

It is so wonderful how He introduces the Holy Spirit to us in John 14:15-17: "If you love me, you will keep my commandments. And I will ask the Father, and he will give you another Helper to be with you forever, even the Spirit of Truth, whom the world cannot receive, because it neither sees him nor knows him. You know him, for he dwells with you and will be in you." I love to read the promises of Jesus, especially when those promises are directly related to our personal relationship with Him. When Jesus promises His Holy Spirit will be in us and at work through us, how can we refuse to be evangelical? How can we in good faith claim Him as Lord and yet never announce His incredible saving promise to a single person in need of a Savior? If we really take these two promises to heart, we must recognize that Jesus implants His Holy Spirit in us so that He Himself will fulfill these promises. Can you imagine Him doing that in and through a person who has no relationship with Him?

I have learned that if a Christian doesn't realize and understand the importance of obedient love, they will never share the Gospel of Jesus or truly come to experience a personal relationship with Christ. Have you ever heard of a monk that after taking a vow of silence had the power of the Holy Spirit pour out of his life? What I am saying is disciples don't remain silent in order to be in a right relationship with God. They certainly don't hide in a mountain monastery or comfortable living room in order to be obedient to Christ's commands. Jesus commands us to make disciples and you can be assured of this: He is not talking about making more silent-lipped pew sitters in the local church.

Please hear this. We do not have to figure out the proper strategy for making disciples, because Jesus lays it out in a very practical and easy-to-follow way. He never says, "build a building" or even "find a meeting place." He simply says, "Follow me! Live with me and learn from my life." He never says to us "If you don't gather a congregation of people, you cannot make disciples." Jesus clearly develops individual relationships with each of His disciples and He starts immediately with a personal invitation for them to be a part of His life, not a part of His congregation.

Jesus never chose an expert in Old Testament teachings or Jewish law to be an important participant in His strategy of disciple making. He never instructs His disciples to bring any or all new converts back to Himself. His primary commission is for His disciples to teach all that He has taught them to new converts. In fact, when His disciples press Him to choose one over others, He does not, leaving them all on equal ground. Am I saying it only takes one to make a disciple? Not at all! What I am saying is it only takes one to get the process started, especially if you work together as a church to make disciples. In my experience, most Christians have determined that disciple making means to educate others in scripture and religious practice and very few Christians see themselves as knowledgeable enough or adequate to teach another.

The natural progression within a healthy church will include people in many different stages of spiritual maturity and relationship with Christ. We only have to study the spiritual gifts of individual Christians and how they function together as one body for the purpose of growing the Kingdom to understand that Jesus intended for us to go out and initiate the process of disciple making and work together as one body to make disciples and educate them in the teachings of Christ. (See Ephesians 4:10-16)

Jesus also never gives us the example of disciple making one day a week. In my opinion, this is a lazy man's ideology that has corrupted the truth of disciple making. Disciple making is an everyday, church-wide activity designed not just to be something a church does in the midst of its fellowship and worship time on Sunday. Daily disciple making is the very purpose for which the church comes together. Worship is an outpouring of our love, honor, and praise to God Almighty. Fellowship is what we do because we love our fellow believers. Disciple making is the work Jesus Christ commands us to do. In short, it is what we do *together* in obedience to Christ's commands.

Jesus never once told the disciples that they would fall under greater judgement because they were disciples. The fear-and-intimidation method of mobilizing the church is not taught anywhere in scripture. Judgment is only fearful to those that have never trusted Jesus and do not know the reality of His grace and forgiveness. For those who have placed their faith in Christ, judgment is an opportunity to shower our Lord with great blessings of our labor as disciple makers. Everything else we gain or accomplish in our own power is merely fuel for the big bonfire.

Rescuing souls and leading unbelievers to place their faith in Christ is the initial step in making disciples and even though many have gone through evangelism courses and it may seem that being a great evangelist is a prerequisite to being a disciple maker, it simply is not. In fact, when Jesus teaches His disciples to evangelize, it is nothing like what is taught in our churches today. Becoming skilled at sharing the gospel has taken complete precedence over understanding one's role in the disciple-making process. Evangelism has become a forced teaching and, while Christians should have been guided into a closer relationship with the person of Jesus, they have become fear stricken that they might not say all the words right when they share the Gospel. As a result, they subdue the Spirit's urging when the time comes to share their faith and, instead, see missionaries and pastors as the ones who are meant to do the evangelism. Sad, but true, and this may well be why the large majority never share their faith with even one person.

Please hear what I'm saying. Together we can all be a viable part of the disciple-making process. When we, as disciples, love Jesus openly without any fear that we may have to win an argument about God or share a perfectly scripted plan of salvation, we are in the perfect place to let God use our relationship with Him to draw nonbelievers to Him through us. Does that mean we must be able to win souls at the drop of a hat? No! Not at all. It means that we must be willing to see that the unbelievers with whom we are sharing the Gospel fully understand the salvation offered to them and God's desire to have a personal relationship with them.

I will never forget a time in my life when sharing my faith was very, very difficult. I shared my version of the Gospel with a young man who lived near me. I stumbled and flubbed my every word. The truth is, I was scared to death that I was going to mess up the Gospel and as a result this man might die and go to hell. I knew only one thing to do. I asked the young man to forgive me for not being able to fully explain the salvation God wanted to give him. I asked him if I could bring someone back tomorrow and talk again. He agreed. I just knew the assistant pastor at my church was the answer. If anybody could say all the words and explain the plan of salvation correctly, it would be him.

The next evening, we visited with Kevin again and the pastor did an outstanding job. He laid it out so clearly a first grader could have understood and maybe even recited it back to us. But Kevin basically said he wasn't ready. Even though he understood the message loud and clear, it would be another six years before he was ready to hear the Holy Spirit calling him to put his faith in Christ Jesus. Yes, this is the same Kevin I spoke of in Chapter 4. What I am trying to say is; God and God alone saves souls. Should we, as disciples, be able to share the Gospel of salvation? Absolutely! But trust me, I have witnessed hundreds of people pray a sinner's prayer and their lives never changed one iota. Remember this: As disciples of Jesus Christ, knowing how to share your faith and personal relationship with Jesus takes high precedence over being a tremendous soul winner. If God the Father is drawing someone to come to know Jesus as their Lord and Savior, it won't matter if you or the pastor of the church says the words. All that will matter is that the Holy Spirit is, in that moment, doing what only He can do.

If you're paying attention, you know I am saying we cannot continue to sit in our pews and Bible study rooms and patiently wait for God to choose to draw someone who has never heard the Gospel into our midst in hopes that this might be our one privileged opportunity to make a disciple. Jesus commands us to go out. We will never experience a full relationship with Christ unless we do. We must make a plan to go out, share our faith, and draw those who receive salvation into our midst and together make disciples. This is the only way we can be obedient to the commands of our Lord in Matthew 28:18-20.

I know the way this world communicates is far different than in the days that Jesus walked this earth but, on the authority of God's Word, I tell you that we must go and be witnesses of God. Acts 1:8 is still relevant today and the truth that Jesus is conveying is that our personal relationship with Him becomes our personal message to a Godless man, woman, country or world. We have to be intentional about sharing it with others. We must be intentional about inviting believers to become disciples, and we must stop giving excuses for why we can't and don't.

In my personal ministry, I have learned that men in particular think everything is fine between them and their God. Because of this, we have to be very intentional about asking them to describe their personal relationship with Jesus Christ. We have to ask them to show us the evidence of their spiritual birth and we have to do so in such a way that they realize it is not from a lofty position that we ask but from one that is genuinely concerned about their spiritual life and growth as children of God. We must invite others to be a part of our lives and become closely related to our daily relationship with Christ.

When we are committed to being intentional about being disciples and inviting other believers to be a part of our lives, we must be prepared for one of the most difficult lifestyles known to man. The Apostle Paul once compared it to the life of a dedicated athlete and the hours and days of intense physical training necessary to run to win. We must be prepared and committed to endure some hard times, some deep personal hurts, and some frustrations with our own abilities to convey our relationship with Christ in a way that compels others to want what we have. We must be willing and disciplined to follow the leading of the Holy Spirit. We will often have to wait on the Spirit to act before we do and we will have to become disciplined to remaining humble and usable in the lives of other believers. We must be committed from the start to train and prepare and continue to go and go until God trusts us and draws that future disciple maker into our lives. Our training and preparation as well as our everyday efforts will be every bit as intense as an athlete forcing their body into race-winning shape.

When I was a young man, my every day was spent working on farms and ranches. It was hard work and often so hot it was hard to think straight. It was hard to keep a positive attitude and not give up or simply drag through the afternoon. At 16, it was hard not to stay in bed late in the morning. It was hard not having time for a favorite TV show. It was hard hearing that farmer yelling foul words, pushing us boys to go faster and work harder. It was really hard on Friday afternoon knowing if you went out with the guys and chased girls late into the night, you still had to get up before daylight and haul hay on Saturday morning.

Those were the most physically demanding days of my life, but because of high school basketball and other sports, I was in top physical shape and even though the work was hard and long, my body could go on cruise mode and endure the struggle with little trouble. Before too long, the work became fun. Today I relate that to my spiritual life and I think back to when I was 29, when God revealed Himself to me and, for the first time in my life, I began to seek a personal relationship with Him. He drew me to Godly men that taught me how to spiritually prepare and to be a disciple of Christ. I had to learn what taking up my cross daily meant and I had to become spiritually fit to endure the task of disciple making.

God sent me on mission to be trained in faith dependence, how to share the Gospel and to serve Him through serving and loving others, including some that didn't even believe there was a God. I say this because I have learned that if we are to have a right relationship on a daily basis with Christ, we have to learn complete and utter dependence on Jesus. Trust me when I say that will not happen as long as we are attached to our comfort zones. Jesus said it best when He told His disciples of the rich man and his shrewd manager. (See Luke 16:1-13.) When our hearts are glued to the material things we own and the places and people in which we find joy and comfort, it is impossible to be dependent on God.

When Jesus sent His disciples on mission, they learned that devotion and dependence on Jesus was the key to experiencing the presence and power of God in their lives. It only took one good mission trip after a year-and-a-half of spiritual preparation to change the lives of these men forever, not in some arrogant way but in a humble, dependent way. While on mission, they learned how much their relationship with Christ was magnified when they got out of their comfort zones and depended on Christ for all things physical, emotional and spiritual. Knowing their greatest need was not toys and comfort food and being in a place where they had access to all of life's comforts allowed them to see that their greatest need was to depend on Christ alone. Going on mission and learning this truth forever humbled them.

I had this same experience when I surrendered my comforts and agreed to go on mission with Christ. I have also witnessed hundreds of faithful Christians make the same choice to obediently go on mission and be spiritually prepared to depend solely and completely on Christ. As a result, their entire lives were humbled and changed. When they returned, the large majority of them became bold witnesses within their comfort zones.

I will never forget a young pastor who brought a team of short-term missionaries to Mexico. He spent at least a month spiritually preparing them to serve in love and share the Gospel. Many great life-changing things happened while they were on this mission, but the one that stood out the most to me was what happened in the life of the pastor's mother. She had come for the sole purpose of cooking for the team. In fact, she had told herself that God had sent her for one reason alone. So every day she stayed back and prepared food for the team. Each night she heard the great stories of how God used the team to draw people to salvation and the more she heard, the more God called her out of her comfortable kitchen.

The last day she gave up and went out with the team. She gave this testimony that night during the team's share time. Through tear-filled eyes she said, "Today, for the first time in my not-so-young life, I led a couple to place their faith in Jesus and commit to make Him their Lord. But that's not the real reason I am here. I believe He drew me all the way to Mexico and empowered my very shy person to boldly share my faith in order to teach me that if I depend on Him, I can go share my faith with my troubled old neighbor man who has lived across the street from me for at least 20 years." God calls His disciples out of their comfort zones but not just for a mountaintop experience. He calls them that He might show them how to walk in the everyday valley of life, how to carry their cross daily, and how to depend on Him in all things.

I learned a valuable lesson through that experience. I believe that every disciple maker must learn and understand how diverse God's plan to evangelize the world is. This grandmother cannot and will never be a missionary to a distant land. However, she is a missionary every day of her life and a valuable part of the disciple-making process. She did go home and she did lead that crusty old neighbor to place his faith in the Lord. I wish I could tell an incredible story of how God used every person I have served with and trained to be a missionary right where God planted them, but I can't. Missionaries must take up their crosses daily and follow Jesus into the white harvest field all around them.

Don't get me wrong. Some people are called to make disciples in far-off, distant lands, and their home churches and brothers in Christ should be helping in their disciple-making efforts. Short-term teams designed to assist and be servants to our career missionaries are vital to their long-term success. However, serving on a short-term team does not negate the need to be disciple makers wherever God has planted you. For that matter, we can all share our faith, lead non-believers to salvation and start the process anywhere we go. Most of our lives will be spent within the small area we call home. It is up to us to choose to be disciple makers where we live on a daily basis or go on mission one week a year and be a part of the disciple-making process of a career missionary. I believe most of us have the privilege of doing both, if we so choose. After all, like we saw earlier, God teaches great lessons when we get away from our comfort zones and depend solely on Him. Never tell God no when His Spirit urges you to go on mission. When we are in a right relationship with Christ, the Father will draw us to where Jesus is already at work. We have the choice to join Him and become a part of the disciple-making process or to disobey.

I found getting started to be a real challenge so here are some **keys to getting started.** My desire in writing this book and *The Carpenter's Guide* is to make your road to becoming a disciple maker easier to grasp. If you haven't already learned, you will soon learn the hardest part of disciple making is getting started. Trying to get started without the prompting of the Holy Spirit is like going deep sea fishing in a rubber kayak. It took me many years to trust the Spirit of God to draw me to those in whom He was already at work. Over and over again I tried to force my way into someone's life because I believed they were like me and wanted to be a disciple as well, when all the while I was the one who had no idea where to start. I would often invite someone to a Bible study and try to use that forum to make them a disciple. I failed miserably. Failure will discourage you much faster than a long wait ever will.

    God used an old-fashioned preacher, J. Vernon McGee, to reveal to me where to start. I began to realize how few Christians understand the conversation Jesus had with Nicodemus and how few men in the pulpit are answering this question. I looked at my own life and realized that even though I prayed to receive salvation as a small boy, I could not identify the evidence of spiritual birth in my own life prior to age 29 when God revealed to me that He wanted a personal relationship with me. The more I recognized Jesus in me, the harder I sought to know Him more. Nevertheless, I am an American and I want everything now. But it was years, as it well may be with you, before God trusted me to be a disciple maker.

    The first person I ever asked to describe his spiritual birth to me was a very intelligent brother in Christ with two theological degrees. He served as associate pastor and the primary Bible teacher in a Southern Baptist Church. I had known him for 15 years or so, served with him on mission teams, and often sought his counsel in spiritual matters. I believed if anyone could give me a straight-to-the-point answer, it would be him. Surprised would be an understatement to his reaction. Have you ever poured ice cold water over the head of a hot, sweaty person's head? That would be a close description of the look on his face.

After a moment or two of staring at me with his jaw dropped open, he said, "I can't believe you're asking me this." I replied, "Why? Of all the men I know, you are the most spiritually connected. You must be the person who can give me the answer." As the pastor, he had not fully taught this truth to his church. In fact, he shared with me that no one had ever even wanted to discuss spiritual birth before. That day I walked away with one very important piece of the plan. I knew one thing for sure: The Spirit was never intended to be a mystery to believers. Jesus taught about the Spirit throughout His ministry and, in John 14, Jesus promises He will be with us and live in us.

I began to study and listen to great teachers on the subject and, maybe more revealing than anything I did, I began to ask brothers and sisters in Christ to tell me about their spiritual birth. Many times I have heard Christians say, "The church house is full of lost people." I fully believe that this is false! Our churches are full of saved Christians who have never been taught to see their own spiritual birth. The American Christian community has done a great job of leading people to put their eternal faith in Jesus, yet we have failed to teach them the most basic of truths that permit each of us to see and live spiritually rich lives.

As disciple makers, we must lead others into a full understanding of our spiritual birth and how to see what Jesus called the Kingdom of God as well as the evidences of that birth and how that grows us in the family of God. This is the foundation Jesus wants us to build on. This is where a relationship with Jesus Christ begins. This is where the understanding of being, living and acting like a child of God begins. We must never assume that the Spirit has revealed its birth to someone and they just know it. This is a copout. This is why you're reading this book and wondering what your spiritual birth looks like. And how can I help someone see their spiritual birth if I can't see my own? Read John 3:1-15 and answer Jesus' underlying question. Have you been born of the Spirit?

I also want to encourage you to study the evidence (fruit), laid out in Galatians 5, and begin to see if those God-given attributes can be attributed to your life. Then start to help other believers see these attributes in themselves. Understand, these do not describe our personalities but rather they identify who lives in us. When we encounter others who have these same attributes, we need to point them out and encourage them to see their spiritual lives from the eyes of God. When we encounter some who do not have these attributes, we should be sensitive to sharing a truth that they will most certainly want.

Another key that is just as important is a **close, personal relationship with Christ.** All Christians who have been born spiritually need a close, personal relationship with Him. They know this and many spend a lifetime in faithful church attendance but never truly experience it in such a way that they can tell about it. Don't think I am being judgmental. I am in no way judging their salvation. What I am saying is their relationship with God is based solely on their time spent in church. They live good, moral lives, treat others with kindness, and avoid problems with fellow believers, while at the same time failing to ever see the power of God in their lives. Those with whom they go to church are their friends but being related to them as a family is simply not something they see as being necessary. Sunday morning worship is where they experience God and fulfill their religious duty. Even so, I believe many of these brothers and sisters are the way they are as a result of what they have learned from someone they saw as an authority in their lives.

So how do disciple makers relate to believers that appear to be very good Christians in every way but don't really understand or care to have a relationship with Christ? I believe we must not judge their lives in any way but, at the same time, we must share our relationship with Christ with them. When God took hold of my life and shook me to my very core, He didn't have to send me a book or a teacher. I was so convicted that I had no real understanding of the Father, the Son or the Holy Spirit that I literally pursued God with a passion.

It is my experience that Jesus draws us and allows us to see another's personal relationship with Him when we are seeking to grow closer to Him and gain greater understanding of the relationship we can have with Him. When we do have a personal relationship with God, He, through His Spirit, will draw us right to the place we need to be in order to be a part of what He is already doing in someone's life. However, I can tell you, as a matter of fact,

He will never draw someone He does not trust to be a part of His relationship with another. As disciple makers, our primary job is to allow our relationship with Christ to be as visible as possible, while at the same time realizing that only God, through His Holy Spirit, can reveal the need for someone to have a close, personal relationship. We must not let our eagerness to help someone have that relationship circumvent the work of the Holy Spirit in drawing someone to Himself through us.

It is our responsibility to teach and lead young disciples into a greater relationship with Christ. And believe it or not, we must follow Jesus' examples in scripture, including His example of leaving our comfort zones and trusting God completely for a period of time. Leading others into a personal relationship with Christ and guiding them into an even closer personal relationship with Him is the work of disciple makers. Others will learn more from spending every minute of every day with us than they ever will in a lifetime of Sunday services. It's up to us to invite them to go with us onto the mission field. We may not be the leader of the mission team, but it is still up to us to walk them through spiritual preparation and help them see the Kingdom come alive in their own lives. We will also be that warrior that says to them, "Watch out! Satan attacks every disciple in this time."

Our complete dependence is required in order to experience transformation. Jesus took His disciples up on the mountainside overlooking a crowd of curious fans and taught them what they would one day know as their lives.

Each one of these men he selected to be a vital part of His strategy and their commitment would cost them everything. If we are to fully commit our lives to Christ, we must embrace the radical changes this will cause in our lives. Paul did a great job of conveying to us what it means here and now, and Jesus revealed the power over the Law that He would give every spiritually-born believer. In Romans 12:1-2, He tells us not to be conformed to this world's standards any longer but to be transformed by the renewing of our minds.

I truly believe Paul had Jesus' Sermon on the Mount in mind when He taught these lessons. When Jesus talked of transformation, He did so with the authority of the only one that can amend the law. The underlying truth is that once Jesus amended the Law, it would never be amended or even edited again. This handful of men's lives would be conformed to these standards through the presence of the Holy Spirit. They, like every new believer, had not yet experienced the power of the Holy Spirit living in them. So, when Jesus started this message with a clear proclamation of the condition of every new believer, He was literally saying to them that, when they received the Holy Spirit, it would be their choice to depend on the Holy Spirit in the same way that an utterly poor person depends on someone else for everything.

The one very distinct difference Jesus made by teaching His disciples separated from, but in full view of, the crowd of people begging for a miracle, was that these amendments would become the dictates of their lives. I believe that during this message He often pointed down at the crowd pointing out the differences in the choices His disciples had made. You see, a disciple commits to follow Jesus and do the things Jesus does until they become like Jesus. The way Jesus teaches this lesson is organized in such a way that the student must understand that in living under this structure, we must fully depend on Jesus and His Holy Spirit that will live in us and one day, through the Holy Spirit, we will be fully transformed into the image of God's son.

It is also very important to note that Jesus was not teaching an unintelligent bunch of laborers. These men, though they may have asked questions, were for the most part fully focused on His every word, soaking it all in. Just like a believer who has experienced spiritual birth, they understood exactly what He was saying. Just look at the crowd's reaction! They were stunned at His teaching, not because they understood it and it profoundly impacted their lives, but because they could not understand it. Yet these common men were literally spellbound by the words of Jesus. And when Jesus got to the house-building section of this lesson, He blew the minds of the super-intelligent Pharisees in the crowd while the disciples fully knew He was ending right where He began, with a strong exclamation point on their full dependence on Him.

Though Jesus' disciples were not a part of the religious leaders, they did have the primary goal of **communicating Christianity** and it was the topic of their lives. No, it was not where the fish were biting. It was Jesus and every word He had spoken, every promise He made, every miracle He performed. In addition, after He sent them out on mission, they returned talking about sharing the gospel and the experiences they had. As disciple makers, we must be so in love with Jesus and sharing His Gospel that we talk about it passionately and with great excitement. We will never lead another to love, commit and put their entire faith in Jesus if we never talk about Him and our personal relationship and experiences in sharing Him with others.

How can someone claim to be a follower of Christ and at the same time is afraid to talk about Him with other believers? Teach your disciples to love to talk about Jesus. Teach them to make Him the center of every conversation. Teach them to never hide their personal experiences and pretend others don't understand. Even if we can see they don't understand; our excitement and passion for Christ will come through and in doing so the young disciple will see the impact his personal relationship with Jesus will have on other believers. Their lives will become evangelical in a very natural way.

Jesus' strategy was **multiplication** from the beginning, but how is it taught and when is a person ready to apply it to his or her life on a daily basis? These are legitimate questions and because it may be the single most important aspect of disciple making, I will give you the answer straight from Jesus' mouth at the moment He called Peter, Andrew, John, and James. In Mathew 4:19, Mark 1:17 and in Luke 5:10, Jesus, calling His disciples for the first time, said to them "Follow me, and I will make you fishers of men." Jesus immediately started teaching multiplication.

Over the past few years, we have been teaching the indigenous people groups in Mexico how to make disciples and we start by teaching them for the purpose of each of them teaching another and teaching that person to teach. This is how we should always approach disciple making. We should never teach or make a disciple for the purpose of educating them for greater status within their communities. When we approach disciple making from the point of multiplication, it changes everything about how we perceive the task. No longer are we out to make a disciple but we are, as Jesus would say, fishing for men.

PERSONAL CHALLENGE

This book reflects my personal experience and its companion study guide, *The Carpenter's Four-Part Guide to Making Disciples,* is a simple tool to get started making disciples. But my guess is that you have many tools and this may just be another to add to a seldom-used collection. Let me tell you, nothing saddens our Lord more than when He reveals truth to us and we store it in our heads and hearts, never to be used.

When you have completed Part 1 of *The Carpenter's Guide*, you will know how to identify your own spiritual birth and that of others. Subsequently, you will be able to focus on your personal relationship with God on a daily basis. As we focus on our personal relationship, we begin to practice identifying the evidences of our Spiritual birth. In particular those listed in Galatians 5:22-23. As this practice becomes a part of our daily activities, it will become habit or second nature to see God's fruits of the spirit in a way that causes us to no longer doubt if God loves us, but thrive in the fruits He has born in us.

Soon, seeing God in the little things of your common day will become treasured and a blessed joy. God will use that joy to draw another person into your life in which He is already working to draw into a personal relationship with Himself. My challenge to every born-again believer reading and preparing to make disciples through this book and *The Carpenter's Guide* today is to act immediately, take the risk, and get involved in what Jesus is doing in that person's life, and let Him use your personal relationship to make a disciple.

When you place your faith over your fear and become related to Christ in His work, you will see Him embrace your participation and a joy will come over you that cannot be equaled in human experience void of the Holy Spirit. In other words, when God's Holy Spirit draws us into His eternal work, He uses that to interact with us on a very personal basis.

I also want to challenge you to do something that will not seem natural to you, but I believe it will change your life and increase your joy level tremendously. Start to view Jesus as a personal loved one. When He draws us into His work, He does so to show us His view of our relationship with Him. His view is letting one of His loved children be a part of His work. This will always be unique to the one to whom He is revealing the relationship.

As we come to see and understand how the God of the universe has chosen to have a personal and unique relationship with us, we begin to realize just how much He loves us. The love He reveals will not just be an understanding of grace. This love will be so natural, so joyous that we will not be able to keep it a secret.

That's where the third challenge I have comes in. Do not hide the love of Jesus in your heart. When your love for Jesus is real and personal, it should and will come out to other believers as if it were as strong as a mother to her little baby or a grandfather showing pictures of his grandchild. I'm not talking about wearing Christian T-shirts and cross necklaces. Those are things that cause us to be noticed but seldom does anyone come to salvation because we advertise our Christianity. This challenge is for you to open your mouth and express your love for Jesus fearlessly. Yes, I challenge you to view your church as a place where you share your loving relationship with God's children. Share what your personal experience really looks like and how God's love has blessed you and I challenge you to share with everyone you meet that you have a personal relationship with Jesus that is filled with more love than any person deserves.

As a final challenge, I use the words of Jesus in Luke 11:2, "When you pray…" Praying is simply what Jesus expects us to do. This Challenge is to get on your knees DAILY and pray for God to draw someone into your life that He wants a personal relationship with. Ask your loving Father to choose to make disciples through you. He promises to be with you and in you. Be obedient to pray before all things and never settle for one disciple-making experience. Ask and keep on asking, go and keep on going, love like Jesus and keep on loving like Jesus.

Suggested Study

Glen D. Pierce, *The Carpenter's Four-Part Guide to Making* Disciples (CrossVision Missions INT, 2016).

Suggested Reading

Robert E. Coleman, *The Master Plan of Evangelism* (Fleming H. Revell, New Spire Edition, 1994).

Robert E. Coleman, *The Master Plan of Discipleship* (Fleming H. Revell, New Spire Edition, 1998).

A.W. Tozer, *The Pursuit of God* (Wing Spread Publishers, 1993).

A.W. Tozer, *God's Pursuit of Man* (Wing Spread Publishers, 2007).

Made in the USA
Charleston, SC
18 March 2016